SUCCESS 1010™
for living

Raimond Volpe

First published 2016 for Raimond Volpe by
Pacific Books, an imprint of
Longueville Media Pty Ltd
PO Box 205 Haberfield NSW 2045 Australia
www.longmedia.com.au
info@longmedia.com.au
Tel. +61 2 9362 8441

Copyright © Raimond Volpe 2016

All rights reserved. No part of this publication may be reproduced or transmitted in any form or by any means, electronic or mechanical, including photocopying, recording or by any information storage and retrieval system, without the prior permission in writing from the authors and copyright holders.

The content and views expressed in this book are of a general nature and are not intended to provide specific advice in relation to individual people or business situations. Readers should always seek their own specific professional advice relating to their situation. The opinions expressed in interviews in this book are personal perspectives of the interviewees only and are not necessarily the views of the author.

ISBN (paperback): 978-0-9945781-0-5
ISBN (eBook): 978-0-9945781-1-2

For the National Library of Australia Cataloguing-in-Publication entry visit www.nla.gov.au

Acknowledgements

I would like to humbly acknowledge my mother Angela for inspiring me to write countless stories as a child and unleash my creative mind. I would also like to thank her for her continual love for me, her ongoing support in writing this book, and especially for letting me use her as a sounding board many times each day during the writing process.

I would like to acknowledge my father Emilio, who taught me valuable discipline and honesty from an early age.

I would like to extend my profound appreciation to Suzanne Burton for her support and assistance.

I am also grateful for the many other people and things, too numerous to mention, which have contributed to my journey in writing this book.

Navigating SUCCESS 1010™ for living

Introduction   1

Part 1
Understanding Success and Stuckburies®

The Meaning of Success   6
Stuckburies®   19

Part 2
Stopping what Stops You from Becoming Successful

The 10 Blockages
1. The Attachment Blockage   32
2. The Emptiness Blockage   47
3. The Intellectual Blockage   57
4. The Depression Blockage   70
5. The Negativity Blockage   87
6. The Victim Blockage   100
7. The 'Shiny Ball' Blockage   112
8. The Stress Blockage   119
9. The Relationship Blockage   129
10. The Struggle Blockage   140

Part 3
Learning to Stay Successful

The 10 Principles to Stay Successful
1. The Crystal Clear Principle — 152
2. The Dynamo Principle — 161
3. The Purposeful Learning Principle — 170
4. The SEV Principle: Select, Expect, Visualise — 175
5. The 'Do Unto Others' Principle — 186
6. The Gratitude & Delayed Gratification Principle — 197
7. The Intuition Principle — 209
8. The Creativity Principle — 215
9. The Taking Responsibility Principle — 228
10. The Self-Analysis Principle — 237

Success1010™ for living
   ... the END and just the BEGINNING — 248

Bibliography and Suggested Reading — 249
Notes — 261

Introduction

Success and happiness are interdependent. You need both to have true success.

I had a major setback in my thirties. Some might call it a breakdown; others might call it depression. It was a setback that lasted six months. Before that, I had always soared through life. I enjoyed engaging with friends and family and making people happy with humour. Sales and human interaction businesses suited me.

I owned my first business at twenty-five and began to run other companies, whilst simultaneously building my own large companies. Without realising it, I was getting mentally fatigued. In my mid-thirties everything fell apart. Mental health, physical health, a long-term relationship, my work, even my own business – everything went downhill at once.

During those six months I could not function. I shut down a thriving business, my long-term relationship ended, and I became somewhat of a recluse. The upside to this was that it gave me time to think, and think hard. How and why had I ended up this way? By most people's definition, I was successful.

I discovered that the mind is the most powerful tool God has given us. When we connect with our mind, it opens us up to the paths we can choose to take in life and what we do. Simply put, what the mind chooses to see, to embrace, colours the actions we take and what we attract into our lives. Success is not the bottom line. Success comes about by way of an effective balance of faith, family, community, and work.

In my case, I was extremely motivated and driven to uncover how I had derailed. I set out on a new journey, to find out why. I rebuilt myself mentally, physically, emotionally, spiritually, and changed my mindset. I became fascinated by successful people and what makes them stay successful.

I started my research, and to this day have never stopped researching the secrets to success and staying successful. Researching and writing this book has taken me ten years.

In doing so, I realised something amazing! We all have blockages. Blockages stop us from being the best version of ourselves and fulfilling our passions and deepest goals and desires. Examining various elements in people's lives, I began to understand what we all have: the elements of faith, family, community, and work; however, we may not be balancing them well.

Our blockages knock us off balance. Falling to such a low point in my life, the lowest I had ever been, turned out to be the best thing that could have happened to me. It allowed me to examine the mind, humanity, happiness, and successful people, and to develop this book so that you can be and stay successful.

We all start the day with a fresh approach. We can all start a new diet to be healthier; we can all go to a motivational seminar ready to start a new life. But what happens a few days, weeks, or possibly months later, is that we stop. We fail to commit long term to our goals.

So, why do we not continue? The answer stems from our *blockages*. These blockages typically start in childhood. This book is designed to help you uncover the hidden traumatic events of your past that have so far shaped your life. These events affect you, yet stay hidden for decades. When they surface and develop in our lives, they subject us to a continual cycle of painful relationships, doubts, fears, and uncertainty.

I needed to write a book about these blockages, how to reverse and eradicate them, so that we can live in happiness – without fear, without regrets, and, most importantly, without guilt.

'Success1010' refers to the 10 primary blockages that negatively affect us along with the 10 principles that, if we apply them to our lives, will help us to overcome these blockages and achieve success.

Success is persisting and striving to grow more. It is approaching fear and going for it. Playing it safe is not growing. Success is all about having the opportunity to grow emotionally, spiritually, socially, financially, mentally, lovingly, and intuitively.

In this book, you will uncover the secrets and methodologies to stop the things that prevent you from starting on your road to success. Once you rid yourself of what is blocking you, you will find yourself eager to kick off your journey to success.

You will feel your creativity launching itself, and feel free and comfortable with your new way of living, whilst adhering to some basic rules and guidelines to maintain you on your path.

The book is broken into three parts.

Part 1 analyses the real definition of success, and its many variations and meanings. Part 1 also talks about the dreaded *stuckburies*. 'Stuckburies' are what I call the traumatic life experiences that occurred in the past, when we were youngsters: traumatic experiences that have shaped our lives and given rise to our blockages – things that have gotten stuck and buried for years.

Part 2 discusses the 10 most significant blockages we may encounter in life and examines the ways in which we can stop being stuck – how to treat and eliminate the blockages that hold us back and prevent us from realising our true potential.

And, finally, Part 3 explores the principles underlying how to stay successful. This is the most uplifting, motivating, and inspirational section of the book, because by now you will have done the hard part. The most important part of becoming successful is not just overcoming your hurdles and reaching that summit but settling yourself there.

When a person goes downhill, it is most likely because of their stuckburies, traumas they may not have yet dealt with. If they have not dealt with their stuckburies, then it is likely they've gone downhill because they lack the tools necessary to maintain the forward trajectory of their successful journey through life.

It is not enough to simply do the work in Parts 1 and 2, to uncover and deal with what's holding you back – you do not want to reach the summit only to find yourself hurtling down the other side.

The magical thing that successful people do that other people fail to do is to take action. They visualise things and then make those things happen. Others may visualise, they may talk, plan, dream, and even organise, just like successful people, but they fail to take action. They talk the talk but never walk the walk. And the reason they fail to walk the walk is because of their fears. This book will show you how to uncover these fears, deal with each of them, and toss them aside. It will show you how to develop resilience and confidence so you can achieve the true success you deserve, the success that is meant for you.

Get ready for an experience that will shape, change, and enable you to experience love, and win the fulfilling successful life that you deserve.

PART 1
Understanding Success and Stuckburies

The Meaning of Success

> *Eighty per cent of success is showing up.*
> — Woody Allen

Have you ever wondered why a man with all the money in the world would continue to strive for more and more money? If he feels empty and unfulfilled, struggling for a valid reason to get up each day, his idea of success is not making him happy. It does not encompass the things in life that will meet his needs and contribute to his fulfilment and happiness. Only the man who feels fulfilled gets up each day eager to make new strides.

The Meaning of True Success – Success1010™

We have heard countless times that money does not guarantee happiness. Money may reduce sadness to a certain extent because it offers one a greater ability and ease to survive. However, research shows that ultimately what brings us happiness is knowing that our time is well spent; time spent enjoyably with others and helping others. The better you use your time, the happier you will likely feel.[1]

Time, not money, is our most precious resource. As such, we should spend it wisely. When we suffer blockages, our time is not enjoyable and relationships with those closest to us are often a struggle. The problem is that blockages hold us back from fulfilling our potential and spending our time in satisfying ways. For example, spending time with the right people, doing the things we are passionate about, and achieving and growing, all centre on spending our time wisely and being happy.

I strongly believe that success breeds success and that goodness breeds goodness. What I mean is that just as witnessing an act of kindness has been shown to create a ripple effect in the behaviour of others,[2] successful people spur other people on to be successful. They are infectious with inspiration. Success-minded people attract other success-minded people.

Think in terms of karma, examining the decisions you make, the choices you have in how you interpret circumstances and the emotions you place on them. For example, when someone says something, we choose how to interpret what they say, whether we perceive it to be good or bad, by filtering it through our past experiences and the biases that have resulted. If someone says, 'That's quite an outfit you're wearing', would you feel flattered? Or would you take it as a criticism? Whether you generally display confidence or feel insecure about yourself colours how you choose to receive such a message.

Our actions result from the way we interpret things and have a direct bearing on our level of happiness. We can choose to change our negative interpretations, the way we see things. Success and happiness are predicated on choice. If you choose to interpret things in a negative or pessimistic way, you are more likely to feel unhappy or dissatisfied.

Let's consider this example. You arrange a date with someone who then stands you up. How does your self-esteem handle that? Do you take it as a personal rejection and wake up the next day feeling subdued and down? Do you shrug it off and instead go visit a friend who is fun to be around, who will lift your spirits? How you cope with it is the choice you make. You choose to either not let it bring you down or dwell in feelings of rejection and misery. Which would you prefer? If you choose anger or sadness over happiness, ask yourself why.

Looking for opportunities in situations keeps you motivated and inspired. For example, if you have been stood up, what lesson can you learn from it and your reaction? By being present, appreciating the moment and the lessons and opportunities each one brings, you can get value from everyone and everything.

There is always a positive, always a silver lining to everything. It is about choosing to find a positive, being determined to find one. Finding the positive generates a feeling of wellbeing. The choice is yours, each and every time.

You might remind yourself that nothing out of your control is guaranteed, that the world is full of surprises. Stuff happens, and not just to you but to everyone. You could choose to accept the person's absence as having nothing to do with you and instead inwardly wish them well in case they could not make it because of circumstances they could not control. By choosing to be kind and understanding, you come from a place of appreciation and kindness, which attracts goodness. When you focus more on what is outside than inside, you make the choice to see things from an entirely different perspective.

Being fully present and conscious of your situation when making decisions employs your heart along with your brain. You not only make better decisions, but also feel better about them. Occupying a positive place, one filled with good karma and happiness, forms the foundation of success.

Successful people come from a positive place. When we are happy, when we feel good about ourselves, we naturally prefer the company of people who are warm, happy, funny, easy-going, honest, and transparent. Successful upbeat people attract likeminded people to them.

Living example of the attractiveness of success

Mirko and Daniel were two different people. Daniel was a glass-half-full kind of guy, a successful professional and enormously popular. Mirko on the other hand lacked confidence and perpetually viewed the glass as half-empty. He saw his life as a constant struggle and complained about the slightest thing to anyone who would listen. The problem was that fewer and fewer people wanted to listen.

Daniel, being easy-going and sympathetic, was always kind to Mirko. Knowing that life was short and that every day was precious, he found himself wanting to encourage Mirko and boost his confidence.

He asked Mirko to a party and Mirko immediately accepted. Daniel was a generous host and his gatherings were always something people looked forward to.

When Mirko arrived, Daniel was surrounded by half a dozen or so friends. He was telling a story and had his friends' full attention. They were smiling and nodding, some chuckling. Mirko felt envy slice through him as he watched how effortlessly Daniel entertained them.

He saw a group of three people standing nearby and joined them. When one of them asked how he knew Daniel, he shrugged and said bitterly, 'I don't know why I come to these things. I think Daniel just throws these parties to show off how successful he is and make the rest of us feel bad'. As his rant continued, two of the three beat a hasty retreat and headed off to mingle with other groups. The third was a woman who had known Daniel for years. She politely interrupted him.

'The Daniel you're describing is nothing like the Daniel I know,' she said. 'He's kind and generous and throws these parties because he loves to bring people together.' When Mirko sneered and began to argue, she gently placed her hand on his arm. 'We can all learn a lot from him,' she said, glancing at Daniel with affection. 'It's hard to resist a smile and a positive attitude. It's downright infectious.' She looked at Mirko kindly. 'You should try it some time.' Mirko stood there speechless as she walked away.

Successful people don't sweat the small stuff and they focus on the positives in situations. Mirko, on the other hand, lived his life in fear, worrying about everything, and feeling victim to every hurdle that presented itself. As a result, even small setbacks seemed massive. Mirko was convinced that life, particularly his life, was grossly unfair and so everything that went wrong reinforced his outlook. He was blocked from experiencing happiness and success by his negativity and feelings of victimisation. Whilst Daniel was living, celebrating life and every challenge that arose, Mirko was stuck. Gratitude and appreciation were things he failed to experience, and so success and happiness continued to elude him.

Getting from down to up, going from a place of disappointment to one of happiness, is critical to success and happiness. However, success is not a destination; it is a journey. In addition, the road to success is always under construction. It is about clearing, reconstructing, and continuing on the journey in order to navigate our way to a happier, more self-fulfilling place. The world is filled with countless opportunities. However, we need to know how to spot these opportunities and be excited by them, not see them as obstacles.

Steve Jobs, with no money, became one of the greatest entrepreneurial success stories of all time.

Jan Koum, CEO and co-founder of WhatsApp, spent a period of his life living on food stamps before Facebook made him a billionaire. Starbucks' Howard Schultz grew up in a housing complex for the poor.

Dr Seuss's first children's book, *And to Think That I Saw It on Mulberry Street*, was turned down by publishers no fewer than 27 times before he convinced someone to publish it. His books have since sold tens of millions of copies. What would the world be like without Thomas Edison? Edison failed hundreds of times over and still persisted.

All of these people have left an indelible mark on our world, and all of them started with little or nothing beyond their commitment and persistence.

Success is about the power to make an impact, a difference in the world. Money was never the goal for these individuals.

Look at former billionaire Chuck Feeney, the duty-free shopping businessman who gave away 99 per cent of his $6.3 billion fortune to help underprivileged children gain an education. He was left with $2 million.

Tony Robbins is arguably one of the greatest self-help gurus and professional development coaches and presenters. He has dedicated much of his life to helping people get motivated and achieve happiness, all the while devoting resources to the underprivileged in over 35 countries, with food donations. Today, his companies continue his work, helping the underprivileged.

We live in an era where spirituality and knowledge create power. The more you learn and connect with the world, the more successful you will become. Having the right mindset to communicate and engage takes practice. Your choice of emotions determines your mindset and behaviour and subsequently determines what and how much action you take.

You are the director of your life. You can choose to create a sad story where you fear relationships and withdraw from others or an inspirational dream that motivates you to connect with people. The art lies in connecting the dots from the opening scene to the closing scene.

Let's view this from a sales perspective. When considering a sales call, for most salespeople, their eye is on the end goal – it is all about closing the sale. They are not spending time thinking of the field that has to be crossed first.

Closing the sale is the easy part. The difficult part is putting yourself out there and asking for the business. The first step is to find a potential client, which takes skill and determination. You can be rejected many times, but you need to trust yourself and keep going.

The second step is meeting with the clients. You need to use various types of engaging techniques to build rapport. There could be multiple meetings. In the journey to attain the sale, you may experience many blockages, such as additional people you need to meet with to gain their approval. Product or service specifications need to be addressed. Once you have done all this and built trust, and done it successfully, passionately, and honestly, you need just ask for the business.

Then, once you get the business, you need to maintain the growth and development of the client. This ensures they are satisfied with your ongoing service and product. Once you have looked after the client, and maintained client retention, you then ask for referrals. The client will give you potential people to contact because you are now a liked and trusted advisor.

Success is not defined by the closing or asking of the business. It comes by way of the hard work expended in positioning yourself to ask for their business. Success is all about the hard yards, the difficulties you must undergo to achieve your end goal.

It is about committing to doing something. It may require change, learning something new. Many of us resist change. Change represents the unknown, and the unknown can generate fear in us if we choose to see the unknown as something to avoid rather than embrace.

Why would we avoid or fear it? That's where our blockages come in. They are responsible for creating that fear. Once we clear the blockage, we can more readily accept and understand the new information.

Have you ever attended a motivating seminar and emerged convinced that you are committed to trying a new path and then, within a few weeks, slipped back to square one again, often without even realising it? What is it that's holding you back?

By working on ourselves to remove our blockages, we can then influence what we have most influence over – us. We do not need our friends or others to make us feel good. We can take the long-lasting road to change. We glimpse what we are capable of, and feel that incredible feeling of strength and growth. This is all part of success.

When we reach this point, success becomes more of who we really are. We start surrounding ourselves with people who are also successful. Being around negative people is not what will make you feel better. This is not about drawing a contrast. Instead, you will find yourself wanting to help negative people to become better, by encouraging them to shed their blockages and move forward alongside you. This forms part of your self-actualisation and your contribution to society, but you do not need to do it in order to feel good about your life.

You will begin to ask the right questions, instead of questioning yourself and others. You will now start to feed your brain from a different information process, one designed to open up your neurological pathways and your mindset to greatness.

The journey to success is well and truly underway when you get more of what you need, rather than more of what you don't need.

Living example of achieving true fulfilment through success

Larry, now in his late thirties, had been overweight since he was a child. He had a good job but he was not performing well. Because of his weight, he struggled with fatigue and crippling headaches that often forced him to take time off work. His doctor warned him that he was going to have to make some significant changes to avert the downward spiral he was on.

Larry turned to his best friend Jane for help. Fit and healthy, she advised him on how to improve his diet and became his informal personal trainer and coach. Steadily, with commitment and effort, Larry turned his life around. He was now feeling good, energetic, for the first time he could remember, and that feeling of wellbeing transferred to the office – he was doing well at his job. Inspired to help others like himself, Larry shared his diet and exercise information on social media. He found that making a difference in people's lives made him feel even more rewarded and fulfilled. Larry was now getting more of what he needed to feel happy, and less of what he did not need.

> Larry's idea of success changed, and now included elements contributing to his wellbeing and happiness. The things Larry had come to believe were important in life, and the goals he now achieved, made him feel happy.

To become happier and more fulfilled, you must be open to expanding your idea of success to include the achievements that contribute to your happiness.

Success means different things to different people. Success aspirations can be personal, relationship-oriented, or professional. Our personal idea of success may be unrelated to markers such as a job title, or relationship status.

- **Subjective success** is viewed from the inside; how you see yourself and your successes. On the professional side, this could include feeling good about accomplishing certain projects, perhaps ahead of deadline or by exceeding expectations, pride in having been singled out for commendation, feeling good about the team you work with or supervise, or simply feeling proud of what it is your company strives for in terms of environmental footprint, quality, mission, customer service, etc.

  On a personal level, subjective success might include being in a strong and supportive partnership/marriage, doing a great job bringing up your kids, feeling good about staying fit, or using personal time to explore and pursue passions and hobbies or contribute to your community in some positive way, such as coaching kids' sports or volunteering at charitable events.

- **Objective success** is viewed from the outside, how others see you. Professional objective success could include how prestigious your job or employer is perceived to be, if you make a substantial salary, are seen as a self-made success, have been publicly presented an award or grant, etc.

Personal objective success might be if you own your home, have had a book published, have been lauded for community service, visibly support your children at school activities or events, or participate in any form of competitive sport, for example.

True success

Much of our own happiness stems from a combination of our values and the events that comprise our individual lives.

Interestingly, the happiness experienced due to life events, such as being offered a dream job, meeting the ideal romantic partner, or achieving a long-term goal, is only short-lived. Apparently, we return to our baseline level of happiness not long after these life events occur.

By putting in place a firm set of values for ourselves, we contribute to the degree of happiness we experience. This experience of happiness is both enduring and stable.

Arthur Brooks, president of the American Enterprise Institute, says that, '…choosing to pursue four basic values of faith, family, community and work is the surest path to happiness, given that a certain percentage is genetic and not under our control in any way.'[3]

Instilling a set of values in your life can help you channel your time into doing things that make you happy. Giving some thought to what truths, what values, resonate with you and then thinking about what kinds of things you can do to adhere to and support those values, and then following through by doing them, will work wonders in generating a great sense of satisfaction in how you are living your life. That satisfaction breeds happiness, which then can spur you on to greater successes.

For example, if you believe staunchly in the importance of supporting your community, you could choose to volunteer at a food pantry, soup kitchen, or youth organisation, just to name a few. Even just a couple of hours a month can make a difference.

If one of your values is to be the best employee/professional you can be, you might consider taking a few certification or college courses or getting a degree that will expand your skill sets and boost what you can offer your employer. The key is to start by analysing what's most important to you and building from there.

Success1010™

How I view true success (or 'Success1010' as I like to call it) is the pursuit of those four basic values – faith, family, community, and work – and shooting for goals that align with those four values. Psychologists use the term 'self-actualisation' to define those who realise their true potential. The ultimate goal in realising one's true potential lies in how we view ourselves, and the things that boost our self-esteem, self-conception, or self-confidence, and requires a clear view of ourselves. Rather than shoot for the stars, the way to succeed at this is to start with the basics, building a foundation, atop which you can construct your path to success.

In 1954, Abraham Maslow published his theory *The Hierarchy of Needs*. According to Maslow, we are motivated by inborn needs that have evolved over tens of thousands of years.

Maslow states that we must satisfy each level of need, starting from the ground up, the lowest level of his triangulated hierarchy. We cannot focus on satisfying the more elevated needs until and unless all the elementary needs are first met. For example, you would not focus on getting an advanced degree immediately if you were not able to put food on the table. You would need to focus on your budget and what you need to do to provide food, shelter, etc., before spending on less immediate issues, and then once those were provided, you can move up to the next step on the ladder.

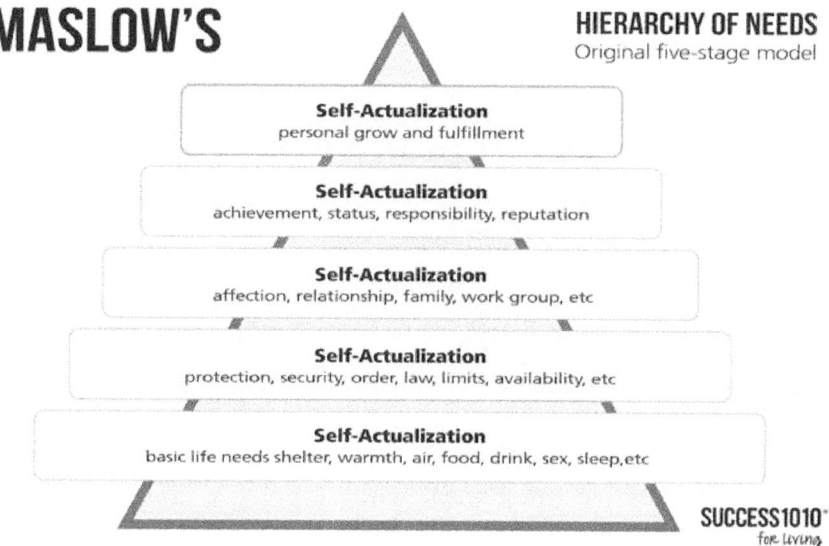

To be successful requires self-actualisation, which, according to Maslow, is the highest level of the hierarchy. So, in order to achieve success, it is necessary to face and overcome the specific challenges at each level of the hierarchy, from the ground up. Only when all these needs are met can true success be attained.

However, that does not mean that we cannot achieve fulfilment until we address all five levels and achieve success. We take it in small steps, solving each problem as we face it and achieving satisfaction at each one.

By solving problems, we feel success is on its way, and this becomes a source of great pleasure and happiness. Problem-free is not a possibility – that's not the goal. Success and happiness come from the sense of satisfaction achieved when dealing with problem after problem, becoming more of who you are, as you progress up the hierarchy of needs. Franklin D. Roosevelt said, 'Happiness lies not in the mere possession of money; it lies in the joy of achievement, in the thrill of creative effort.'

As we progress through the coming chapters, you will see how success and happiness go hand in hand, and how 'Success1010' contributes to an enduring sense of happiness and fulfilment.

SUMMARY

- Research shows that money does not make us happy. What makes us happy is how we spend our time. For example, if we are wasting time, not using time productively, and continually doing things that we don't love, then we may find it difficult to be happy.

- Financial success leads to happiness only up to a certain level of income; after that point happiness increases little, if at all.

- Success is interlinked with happiness. People derive satisfaction and happiness by solving problems.

- Establishing and following a set of personal values leads to a lasting experience of happiness. 'Success1010' stems from achieving goals in the pursuit of the four basic values: faith, family, community, and work.

- Success is about the power to make an impact, a difference in the world.

- Intuition is our most reliable source of information for decision-making.

- The more you learn and connect with the world, the more successful you will feel.

- Self-actualisation lies at the pinnacle of our needs and reveals our true potential. A clear view of ourselves is needed to achieve self-actualisation.

Stuckburies®

> *Whether you think you can or you think you can't, you're right.*
>
> Henry Ford

Our motivation to achieve new goals comes from our idea of having a better life: our ideal self, living in an ideal world. We often daydream about how much better life would be if our circumstances were different: if we had our own business, if we had a better job, if we were more skilful, or if we were in a more loving relationship. Yet when we try to succeed, we often end up failing instead.

Emotions are normal. As humans, we all experience them. And during times of acute stress, they can intensify. At those times, our feelings and emotions can be so full-on that we can find life not only challenging but almost unbearable.

When we are stuck in life, we feel emotionally drained, and life looks doomed. Why and from where do these feelings arise? Often, they derive from our traumatic interpretation of early childhood events. This interpretation is unconscious, as is the way we learnt to cope with the trauma. These events and how we learn to cope with them shape our lives, impacting our future.

'Stuckburies' are unresolved emotional complexes – for instance, our emotional baggage – buried deep within us, which inhibit us from giving our best shot at achieving success.

A stuckbury is most often formed early on in life, typically from infancy through to age seven, but it can form even whilst still in the womb, and also beyond age seven – any time a traumatic event is experienced.

The stuckbury stays with us, in our unconscious mind, as we approach adulthood. In adulthood, as we face new experiences, the stuckbury causes us to unconsciously expect things to be traumatic, just as they were when we were young. We treat new life experiences as though they, too, will turn out the way past childhood experiences did. This is how the stuckbury influences our adult behaviour; we apply our old childhood coping strategies to our new experiences in life.

The word 'stuckbury' was coined by combining two words, 'stuck' and 'buried'. Something buries itself deep within us for many years, the result of a traumatic experience that yields a complex set of emotional reactions, causing us to form blockages in our life. Those blockages leave our lives 'stuck', where we find ourselves experiencing the same problems over and over again, whether it is in relationships, how we handle pressure, decision-making, etc. And the only way to shed these recurring, worsening problems is to take measures to become unstuck. That means digging deep to uncover these stuckburies, to see them for what they are, accept that they happened and why, and then take steps to move past them so they no longer hold us back.

For example, if a child was abused, he or she may develop a strong fear of intimacy or close relationships, convinced they lead to painful experiences. As an adult, this may result in a blockage developing, such as attachment or negativity, where the person has difficulty with intimacy or avoids intimacy, believing that people are no good. The abuse as a child is the trauma trigger and the child's interpretation of the why of this abuse is the stuckbury. As the child becomes an adult, the fear of intimacy is the subsequent blockage that arises from that unconscious stuckbury or belief.

Most of us have blockages in some form or another. It is necessary to address them in order to resolve the problems that arise later in life because we still hold onto them.

There are 10 common blockages that people experience as a result of their individual stuckburies and we deal with these in Part Two:

1. Attachment   5. Negativity   9. Relationship
2. Emptiness   6. Victim   10. Struggle
3. Intellectual   7. 'Shiny ball'
4. Depression   8. Stress

The yearning we have within us for a better life fuels our strong desire for success. Unfortunately, the effort to transform our lives for the better is shadowed by doubt.

Every day we see people struggling to succeed in various aspects of their lives. Despite their best efforts, many of them fail, and continue to fail. Of the countless people attempting to improve their circumstances in life, how many succeed? More importantly, how many of them fail to give themselves credit for the successes they do achieve and instead focus on the negative, what still lies out of reach, the goalpost that perhaps keeps moving, preventing them from achieving their definition of success.

The fear of failure in this sense is the sauce that makes success so much sweeter. The Pareto Principle, named after Italian economist Vilfredo Pareto, and also known as the 80/20 rule, states that, for many situations, 80 per cent of the yield comes from a mere 20 per cent of potential sources, so that 80 per cent of one's achievements come from merely 20 per cent of the time invested. So, as a salesperson, 80 per cent of your sales would typically come from just 20 per cent of your customers.

Although there are many reasons why people fail, they all have a common denominator: the 'emotional roadblock', a psychological illusion stemming from our fears and doubts that prevents us from succeeding. These emotional roadblocks are stuckburies.

Blockage example – stress and depression

Growing up, Alex's parents continually compared him to other children. They wanted Alex to be competitive, so that he might become an accomplished child they could be proud of. Instead, Alex grew up convinced that he would never measure up, that he was never good enough. No matter what he achieved, his parents never seemed satisfied, always urging him to do more, to achieve more, to accomplish more. And because his parents never seemed satisfied, Alex was convinced that he fell short in the eyes of others as well.

As an adult, Alex was still subjected to his parents' relentless comparisons with those who were on impressive career tracks, already owned their own homes, had started families. Although Alex was not married and did not own property, he was in a stable relationship and had a steady job.

Reinforced by his interpretation of how his parents saw him, Alex secretly believed he was not as good as his peers. His magnification of the achievements of others was coloured by his own self-perception. Because Alex doubted himself, he assumed others doubted him too. He became more and more melancholy.

One day during a heated discussion with his partner, Alex fainted. Soon the blackouts became more frequent, until finally Alex sought treatment. He was diagnosed with severe anxiety and depression. These blockages developed from Alex's stuckbury, his belief that he would never be good enough to earn his parents' respect.

Specifically, blockages are a set of reactions that develop in people who have suffered from ongoing stress or a traumatic experience. People with these blockages avoid getting involved in activities that risk triggering the stuckbury upon which the blockage is based.

The earlier the stuckbury is formed, the more severe the blockage that develops. It can be based on a single traumatic event or a series. It also depends on the severity of the trauma and the individual's personality traits.

Imagine a small child who gets lost, separated from its mother. Traumatised, a child might panic and develop a stuckbury, which then becomes a stress or attachment blockage later in life. Yet, when famous entrepreneur Richard Branson was a child, his mother left him in the middle of nowhere to find his way back home. Richard Branson succeeded in finding his path home, learning that he had the ability to overcome difficulty rather than being traumatised by it.

Everyone harbours stuckburies of one kind or another, to varying degrees. During our formative childhood years, emotions dominate and influence our thinking. We use our emotions to try to make sense of the world around us. Sigmund Freud, around the turn of twentieth century, proposed that early childhood experiences have a significant effect upon the adult years of a person's life. Freud's theory that early childhood (infancy to age seven) experiences affect a child's development and influence behaviour throughout adulthood is still widely accepted in the field of psychology today.

According to psychologist Erik Erikson – who worked with Freud – and his theory of psychosocial development, which investigates the way a child comes to understand itself and its relationships with others, dilemmas arise at stages throughout life. These need to be resolved so that the personality can develop. The first stage occurs in the first year or so of life. Stability and consistency of care by the mother leads the infant to develop a sense of trust. The child comes to expect and trust that other people will be caring and supportive too. If the child receives inconsistent and unreliable care by the mother, it inhibits the infant from developing this level of trust, and the mistrust and fear that develops affects its future relationships and situations.[4]

John Bowlby worked as a psychiatrist with emotionally disturbed children in the 1930s, and believed that the critical period for the child's development is 0–5 years of age. He observed that a child's relationship with its mother is important for the child's emotional development, and that early separations from the mother leads to developmental difficulties later in life.[5]

The attachment theory posed by Dollard and Miller in the 1950s states that attachment develops as a result of a group of learned behaviours, originating in our infancy, based on who provides us food. An infant becomes attached to the person who feeds it.[6] Infants associate 'the comfort of being fed' with the person feeding them. The infant also learns that 'certain behaviours (e.g., crying, smiling) bring desirable responses from others. Because of this, they repeat these behaviours, as they know good things will come.[7]

We learn based on our experiences in our early years, and what we learn affects how we perceive the future and whether we have confidence in our own ability to influence events. The stuckbury, originating from childhood events, becomes a blueprint used to perceive and understand current and future relationships and situations.

The following example of a baby and its mother provides an example of the way in which a stuckbury forms, potentially causing an attachment blockage to develop.

> *A baby is regularly put to bed at 9.30am, and sleeps soundly until about 11:30am, a well-established pattern that allows its mother time to get some household chores done. When the baby wakes up, the mother picks the baby up, pampers it, feeds it, and changes it. Because of the consistency of the mother's care, the baby feels secure and content. It has learned to expect and trust that its mother will be there when it wakes.*

> *The mother starts an intimate relationship with Charlie, her neighbour next door. She visits him in the morning when the baby is asleep.*

> *Now, when the baby cries when it wakes, the mother isn't always there to respond immediately. The baby becomes distressed and frightened due to the mother's frequent absences. Because the baby doesn't experience its usual routine, it feels abandoned by the mother and the trust*

that has been learned has now been damaged. Because the baby does not know that the mother is next door and that she will return at some point, its fear is traumatic.

These experiences become the basis for a complex set of anxieties, a stuckbury, which can negatively impact the baby for the rest of its life.

How to unblock

Emotions, stuckburies, and blockages are largely responsible for whether we fail or succeed. The failure versus success rate can be seen in various aspects of our society, for example, marriage and small business. Statistically speaking, nearly half of all married couples in Australia are now expected to end up separated or divorced.[8] The same statistic applies to small businesses, with half of those new businesses closing their doors just a few years after start-up.[9]

We are born with eight primary emotions wired into our heads.[10] All other emotions stem from these eight:

- Sadness
- Happiness
- Fear
- Surprise
- Anger
- Shame
- Disgust
- Interest

We can also experience secondary emotions, emotional reactions to our emotions. For example, if you feel guilty about something, that may make you angry. When experiencing a secondary emotion, it is important to determine the primary emotion in order to understand where from and why the emotion has arisen.

Acceptance and exploration are critical to getting to the root of our stuckburies so that we can eliminate and treat them and the resulting blockages. The more accurate your early identification is of what is holding you back and why, the more precise the questions you can ask yourself. The better the questions you ask, the better the answers you will get, and the better the resources will be to begin the fixing and unblocking process.

To resolve a stuckbury requires that you look at its symptoms, the blockages you repeatedly find yourself facing in life. For example, if you fear change, and this is an observable pattern that prevents you from taking action in life, it is invariably the result of a stuckbury. The first step in determining the cause for this blockage is to recognise this pattern and accept that it exists.

We may not be able to remember how a stuckbury originated, but by identifying our blockages we attune ourselves to the existence of a specific problem. Once we pinpoint the blockage, we can work back to what the stuckbury might be.

Remembering such things is rarely easy or straightforward. You may have suppressed a traumatic memory or been too young to recall or even comprehend the situation. If family members cannot help you, you may want to consider sourcing a licenced therapist for help. One thing is certain. By actively working to uncover stuckburies and eliminating blockages, you will be far better off. Once you clear a blockage, you should see a remarkable improvement in your life.

Regulating feelings is not easy, but by learning to control our emotions rather than being controlled by them, we can enhance our lives remarkably. Controlling and regulating our emotions also gives us the ability to build healthier relationships, both professionally and personally.

Sometimes we regulate the way we feel without even knowing that we are doing it. For example, being around someone positive can lift our spirits the same way being around someone negative can bring us down. Our body language and physiology changes. We can be influenced by the emotional states of others even if we only have an indirect association. Being aware of this is the first step to changing it.

Emotions, thoughts, and behaviours are all linked. A cycle of emotions generates thoughts that lead to feelings that influence how we behave. When we feel doomed or down, we get involved in old patterns. We may use destructive coping strategies, like self-sabotage, unhealthy living, and general harm to our lives.

Emotions are linked to behaviours. For example, if you feel stressed, you may feel the urge to eat or smoke. Some people get angry, so they start blaming, whilst others, when they feel guilt or despair, play the victim. We have the power to choose how we cope.

Emotion	Unconstructive action	Constructive action
Guilt	Close off to the world; see oneself as a victim	Engage more; overcome by addressing it head on
Frustration	Fight/attack	Evade, breathe, display generosity
Pessimism	Give up	Become more social, smile, laugh, give to others

When we elect to tackle our negative reactions in more constructive ways, it enables us to switch the way we feel, from bad or depressed to more engaged and happier. Whilst easier said than done, it is possible. Let's look at some techniques that can help get to the root of our blockages.

Free association

Free association is a method Freud used in place of hypnosis to explore the causes of anxiety or complexes in his patients, and is still used today by psychotherapists and psychoanalysts. In free association, the patient allows his or her mind to wander from thought to thought, and at the same time verbalises these thoughts to a therapist.

The premise of free association is that certain topics are repetitive and revealed by the patient's comments when free associating. Underlying this repetition are the emotionally charged and unconscious psychological complexes: our stuckburies.

The role of the therapist is to notice the repetitive content and link it with the patient's underlying stuckburies. The therapist interprets or verbally reflects back to the patient the link between the patient's thoughts and where they may be getting stuck. This process works towards bringing the stuckbury to the patient's conscious mind, and weakens it over time. Writing down your thoughts and feelings whilst free-associating will also help you to tap into and find out the cause (stuckbury) for your blockage.

Behaviour therapy

Behaviour therapy uses techniques to break down the link between unproductive behaviours and the triggers for these behaviours. For example, if your blockage causes you to chronically arrive for work late, behaviour therapy can uncover the trigger for this behaviour. It might be a fear of success, or of succeeding in your job, so you self-sabotage by arriving late every day. Behaviour therapy focuses on techniques that help alleviate your fear of doing well at your job, removing the trigger for your self-destructive behaviour.

The aim of cognitive-behavioural therapy is to teach you to take charge of your feelings by taking charge of your thoughts. Your therapist helps you to identify your unhelpful or negative thoughts and how they affect the way you feel. The therapy teaches you strategies to combat these unhelpful thoughts, and how to think more constructively.

For example, if you persistently think that your relationship or job is doomed to fail, no matter what the actual circumstances are, then this is the manifestation of a stuckbury. Cognitive behavioural therapy educates you about your patterns of thought, helps you to notice the patterns, and teaches you how to stop thinking this way and instead think more positively. With this new way of thinking about your relationship influencing your behaviour, the relationship is more likely to succeed.

Set SMART (specific, measurable, attainable, realistic, and timely) goals to change your behaviours and reward your repeated successes. This helps you to stay motivated. For example, a person living an unhealthy lifestyle could start by making sure they get to bed on time before moving on to eating a healthier diet. One small goal, once accomplished, leads to setting another, and then another, and the resulting progress gathers momentum. By regularly reviewing and rewarding your progress, small gains will motivate you to achieve more and more.

Discuss the ups and downs of your progress with your therapist or confidant. This instils confidence in your achievements as well as providing you with support. But avoid dwelling upon your problems or blockages excessively, as focusing on them can inflate your perception of them and minimise your achievements. Keep them in perspective and accept their existence without indulging them as you continue to move forward.

SUMMARY

- Everyone harbours stuckburies of one kind or another. It is the common denominator in the reasons we fail, a psychological illusion created from our fears and doubts that blocks us from being successful.

- Stuckburies are the unresolved emotional complexes (emotional baggage) buried within us. A stuckbury is generally formed early on in life, and stems from our interpretation of one or more traumatic experiences in early childhood events.

- Blockages develop from stuckburies. To be successful in life we need to find and eliminate our stuckburies and the blockages they formed that prevent us from realising our true potential.

PART 2
Stopping what Stops You from Becoming Successful

The 10 Blockages

Blockage 1: The Attachment Blockage

> *The purpose of our lives is to be happy.*
>
> Dalai Lama

Have you ever witnessed people who seem unable to operate on their own? They cannot function without their partner/friend/dog/phone, etc. These people suffer from an attachment blockage, which is not uncommon.

The primary caregiver

The primary carer–child bond is a powerful force in infant development. According to attachment bond theory, which was pioneered by English psychiatrist John Bowlby and American psychologist Mary Ainsworth, the relationship between an infant and its primary caretaker:

- shapes our future relationships,

- influences our ability to focus, be conscious of our feelings, and our ability to stay calm when necessary, and

- influences our ability to bounce back from misfortune or hardship.

Children are first exposed to a loving relationship via their primary caregiver, which most often is their mother. As the mother and infant relationship evolves, it has a large bearing on a child's confidence. An understanding of the attachment blockage gives parents the opportunity to more positively impact their children's lives.

The bonding with your mother began with non-verbal communication – holding, stroking, feeding, and other similar nurturing interactions. It was your first emotional relationship and lies at the root of how you interact with people.

Attachment to objects

Young children who lack sufficient bonding experience often shift their attachment to objects such as a doll or, as we see in Charles M. Schultz's *Peanuts* character Linus, a security blanket.

If a child does not receive comfort and safety from their caregiver, they turn to the inanimate object for solace – something that will not leave them and over which they have more control, making them feel more secure.

Attachments in adulthood

The way we react to our peers, partner, or our boss, for example, all relate to how we first experienced emotions like sadness, anger, regret, or grief and how we connected and communicated with our caregiver.

Living example of an attachment blockage

Suzie is 35, married, with a successful career that requires her to travel. As a child, Suzie lived in a perpetual state of anxiety, always feeling the need to care for others. This eagerness has served her well professionally, as her clients feel valued by the level of attention she gives them.

Suzie's husband also requires a great deal of Suzie's attention. He is insecure and is not happy unless she is nearby. He resents how much she enjoys her solo trips because she does not seem to need him the way he needs her. He fears that one day she will leave him. As a result, he manipulates her to get attention, often exaggerating his health needs, exploiting her fears by claiming his problems are exacerbated by her absence and neglect.

Suzie is torn between the joy that her job gives her and wanting to care for her clients and her fear and guilt that her husband is not able to cope properly when she leaves his side. She feels torn between her responsibilities.

Each suffers from an attachment blockage. Suzie cannot progress with her life because she allows herself to be manipulated through guilt whilst Suzie's husband cannot bear not to have his wife by his side.

An attachment blockage is a *restrictive emotional response* that inhibits our behaviour and relationships.

Causes

Neglect is arguably the most common root of attachment blockage, where a child's primary caregiver is too busy or unavailable to devote sufficient time to attending to the child's needs. The child may grow to avoid close relationships because they view the emotional links as painful or unreliable.

Another common cause is where parents are not consistent in their approach to their children. For example, reacting differently from one day to the next. The children have not changed or done anything different, but the parent's behaviour is erratic and so the child becomes confused and uncertain, anxious because they cannot figure out how to behave in ways that would encourage consistent, positive support.

An insecure attachment early in life may often reveal itself in later adulthood as an attachment blockage. Examples include needing to be in a particular person's company all the time and having that person's undivided attention, or an inability to make decisions without that person's approval. This blockage makes it difficult for us to function independently, either slowing our personal progress down or blocking it altogether so that we feel trapped.

These unhealthy attachments may appear in any area of our lives, for example in our romantic relationships, or with our family. A healthy attachment, on the other hand, provides us a secure environment in which to persist and strive for success.

How attachment blockages affect success

With an attachment blockage you lack sufficient confidence to do things on your own, including making decisions. Decision-making skills are necessary to progress, whether it be investments, resources, relationships – whatever. When you allow other people to make your decisions, you hand your power and independence over to them, which is not the path to success.

To grow as a person, we need to learn from our decisions and mistakes. When someone else decides for us, that is passive, and we miss the opportunity to learn. If you choose not to study for an exam and instead have your friend take it for you, aside from the obvious ethical issues, you short-change yourself because you have chosen not to learn what you need to know. If you do not know the fundamentals, how can you build on anything? That independence, that willingness to take a risk and make a mistake, is the foundation upon which success is built. How can you succeed when you avoid trying? If, for example, you are in business and dependent on your partner to make all the necessary decisions, it could be hard for you to stay in business if the partner relationship dissolves.

If you are on the receiving end of an attachment blockage, meaning that the person you are dealing with has the blockage, they will inevitably attempt to manipulate you in order to get their needs met. Such manipulation can, and likely will, prevent you from growing and moving forward in your life.

People desperately want to remain close to the people they are dependent upon. In relationships, they feel they cannot leave behind the partner they feel attached to.

People can also display obsessive attachments to possessions and places. The reason they cannot let go is their attachment to their emotions. They feel down, due to safety and insecurity issues. They have little confidence. They have given their power to the people they are dependent on. Letting go of the attachment enables these individuals to move forward into the next stage of their life.

Fear and safety

Fear of change and the unknown often makes people establish a secure comfort zone and plant themselves rigidly inside it. For example, a person may decide to stay in the town they grew up in, rather than leave to experience fresh challenges. Instead of taking a risk to fulfil their potential, they purposely limit their future opportunities so they can remain safely within that comfort zone, where nothing threatens their sense of security.

How attachment blockages form

An attachment blockage comes from an inner unconscious belief that your identity is intertwined with that of the person who you feel attached to. So, in effect, you feel that their fate is also your fate. This is called *enmeshment*, where you are not clear about where your responsibilities begin and end. In order to overcome this, it is necessary to understand the boundaries surrounding the responsibilities and control in your relationship.

Addressing the attachment blockage

Recovery involves a solid reversal of patterns in order to reconnect with and differentiate yourself.

For a balanced relationship, control and responsibility need to be in alignment. Alignment occurs when a person takes responsibility for something within their control and does not attempt to assume responsibility over something that is not within their control. When *control* and *responsibility* are not aligned, distress is the inevitable result.

In our living example of an attachment blockage, Suzie has taken undue responsibility for her husband's welfare, happiness, and wellbeing. Suzie needs to break the blockage. Unless such a fundamental paradigm shift occurs, they will both continue to feel stressed.

Understanding and recognising your attachment patterns

Do you find yourself feeling hesitant, or even scared, every time you are expected to function without supervision? If so, your first step in overcoming this is to work out how this developed. Knowing what you know now about how a child develops attachment blockages, use that to isolate what, if any, security issues you felt as a child towards your parent/caregiver. Once you can identify your stuckbury and how it evolved, you can begin accepting its presence and influence in order to move forward and overcome it.

Triggers

The next step is to identify and recognise when your attachment blockage surfaces. People can look fine on the outside, however, within themselves they may be churning with anxiety, anger, fear – any number of stress-derived emotions. Once you work out what types of situations trigger your blockage, you can start addressing the trigger. Learning as much about your attachment blockage as you can will enable you to exert more influence over it. By fixing it, the better your life will be, and you will feel a level of power and strength you may have never experienced before.

If you are unable to progress in identifying and overcoming your personal stuckbury, you may want to consider consulting a licenced therapist, preferably one who is familiar with attachment blockage and is willing to incorporate this into a therapeutic approach.

Find people with secure attachment styles

Many self-help sources recommend surrounding yourself with a strong support system, two or three individuals who are positive-minded and encouraging, and are willing to be there for you when you need a nudge or just a sounding board. They must also pledge to be honest with you and not just tell you what you want to hear.

A supportive source needs to be someone who does not suffer from the same blockage, because someone with a similar blockage may not be able to see the situation quite as clearly. If you have a close friend or partner suffering from an attachment blockage, your relationship is likely co-dependent and so, by definition, they will not wholly support you changing. In fact, they are more likely to try to talk you out of it.

Like any challenge, this kind of progress takes time and plenty of patience, both with the process and with yourself. Take it slowly. There's an old joke that goes: *How do you eat an elephant?* The answer is: *One bite at a time.*

Take heart. According to the experts, roughly half of all adults are secure in their attachments. And much like being with upbeat cheery people lifts your spirits, surrounding yourself with people who do not experience undue fear in their relationships with other people can, over time, bolster your own confidence.

On paper

When you can identify the advantages of living without an attachment blockage, it may further motivate you and speed up your ability to overcome it. Much like the benefits of sitting down and listing the pros and cons of a decision in order to see them in black and white, you may find it helpful to spend a little time pondering the pros and cons of addressing an attachment blockage. Try to phrase your pros and cons using 'I' statements.

Here are a few examples to get you thinking more about it:

Pros of tackling my attachment blockage.

- I will feel more independent.

- I will be more willing to make new friends and improve my relationship with my existing friends and family.

- I could make myself more eligible for a promotion at work because I will feel more secure in working independently.

Cons of tackling my attachment blockage:

- My relationship with my partner might end if they resist my changing.

Behaviours

Once you identify the advantages in overcoming an attachment blockage, you will find yourself eager to make progress. Most of your attachment blockages will reveal themselves in your behaviour, in your kneejerk reactions and how you cope with various situations. Start by examining situations where you experienced anxiety in your relationship with someone and jot down notes on what happened, how you reacted, what the other person may have said, and how that made you feel, and how you responded. Be honest with yourself. These are your private notes and not for anyone else's eyes, so be as objective as you can. And whilst you are reliving the situation, note whether the memory of any particular words, actions, or circumstances make you feel stressed and anxious as you recall them. All of these are valuable clues that will help you to move forward and choose to react differently in the future.

The next step is to consider alternate, healthier ways that you can react to such stressful situations.

For example, if you feel lonely when your partner is not with you, try activities you enjoy that absorb your attention to the point where you do not notice their absence. If you love to read, pick up the latest bestseller and dive in. If you enjoy gardening, go out and get your hands dirty. Take a painting or dance class. If that does not do it for you, consider volunteer work. Focusing on the needs of others is the best way to not just forget about our own troubles for a while but also make us feel gratitude for what we have in our lives.

Setbacks

As you progress, you may find yourself occasionally slipping back into old habits. It is easy to lapse back into old ways of doing and reacting to things. Don't beat yourself up about it but by all means do something about it. If it is helpful, post reminder notes where you can see them. If you tend to wake up feeling agitated or uneasy, a few inspirational quotations stuck to the bathroom mirror will remind you that you can consciously change your outlook. It is your choice to see the glass as either half-empty or half-full. But success comes to those who see it as half-full.

Think about the successes, the achievements you've already accomplished so far. This is called 'achievement and appreciation analysis'. Looking at how much you have achieved gives you the confidence you need to pick yourself up. By reminding yourself of your goals, of what you stand to gain when you make these changes, you can see how many wonderful things are waiting for you at the finish line. Before you know it, you are moving forward again.

Self-acceptance

When you begin to make progress, it is tempting to think that the problem has now been resolved and is no more. But, as the saying goes, old habits die hard. As mentioned earlier, it is important to recognise and accept the existence of your stuckbury in order to move past it. It is also important to accept yourself for who you are, strengths and weaknesses, and do so without attaching any feelings of remorse, guilt, anger, defeat, or even arrogance.

Why? Because when you start to feel bad, you self-sabotage. You start making yourself feel worse through guilt, blame, and thoughts of weakness. When you accept who you are, you can be kind to yourself, instead of cruel. And when you think kindly of yourself, you are more inclined to think kindly of others.

Instead of blaming everyone else, you now voluntarily take responsibility for your own actions. Wait, or work out a Plan B. (At the end of Blockage 4, I list eight Plan B options that I use.) Having a Plan B is great. You do not have to carry it out to feel better. It is comforting just to know it is there in case you need it.

Knowing I have a Plan B has been so powerful for me; it has turned me from a bundle of sadness to a bundle of joy in minutes. There were two reasons. When you practise self-acceptance, and use a Plan B as a contingency, you learn that:

- A Plan B gives you an option to get out of pain, and

- You overcame your co-dependency issue within a short time frame and you did it yourself with your thoughts.

Self-acceptance allows you to forgive yourself and others for actions more readily. As your confidence grows, you become more self-reliant, less dependent on others for your validation. You can start looking at yourself honestly, objectively, without excuses or feelings of inadequacy.

There is another benefit to tackling your attachment blockage and developing self-acceptance. Healthy people naturally draw other healthy people to them, while unhealthy people tend to attract similarly unhealthy people. If the people you attract also suffer from attachment blockages, they may see you as a target to push around in an attempt to make them feel better about themselves. By becoming more in tune with yourself, and more self-reliant, you will no longer feel susceptible to the destructive actions of these people. By accepting yourself, you will see their actions more clearly, more objectively, as having nothing to do with you. It takes time; it does not happen immediately. But eventually you will have a *No Standing* sign on you when these people approach. They will not linger when they discover they can no longer push you around.

It is an exciting journey, the journey to self-acceptance and self-actualisation, but it is important to recognise that your relationships with the people around you, including your loved ones, are going to change. That can be disconcerting, even saddening, but you must remind yourself that you are equipping yourself with the skills to attract healthy people. If loved ones fight against the changes you are making, step back, accept them for who they are (and the blockages they are likely suffering from), and let go. Those who truly love you will remain.

Trying new things involves risk, but it means you are getting to know yourself better all the time, and that is progress. You are getting the relationship with yourself back. When you do nothing and stay the same, you are playing it safe. But when has playing it safe ever moved you forward?

If you are unsure about the progress you are making, then it is time to break it down. Focus on one relationship you are determined to improve and for one week set yourself the goal to move it forward. At the end of each day during that week, ask yourself how you did. For example, if you are struggling to overcome your fear of working more independently and not relying excessively on your boss, you might do this:

Goal: *To stop relying on my boss to direct my every action; to be more independent; to not feel anxious when he/she is not immediately reachable.*

Daily Question: How did I manage my attachment blockage with my boss today?

Your responses might look something like this:

Day One: She left the office for three hours and I felt anxious the entire time. I couldn't get anything accomplished until she returned and I was able to talk to her about what I was working on.

Day Two: She was locked in meetings all day. I scribbled a note to myself on my desk reminding me that I can cope on my own, but I still felt anxious most of the day. I was not as productive as I should have been.

Day Three: She gave me an assignment and instead of peppering her with questions, I took a deep breath and tried to tackle it on my own. It was stressful but it turned out that most of my questions were ones I was able to get the answers to myself. So, whilst I felt anxious, I felt I made a little progress and it felt pretty good!

Day Four: I felt calmer today, until two o'clock, when she went into a meeting and a minor crisis arose. I know I should have been able to deal with it myself but I panicked and pulled her out of her meeting. She was annoyed and I felt depressed. I left a note on my desk for the morning with a new goal: to not contact her with any questions, no matter what, before three o'clock.

Day Five: I can't believe it! I actually got through the entire day without having to ask her advice on anything! I did it! I think she noticed, because she smiled as she was leaving for the day and wished me a good weekend. I am setting myself this same goal for next week and am determined to do better. For the first time in I can't remember when, I felt happy when I left the office.

Change yourself, not others

You cannot change other people. All you can change is how you choose to react to them. In becoming more self-reliant, you release your need for people to behave in certain ways. Focus on your own journey. By that, I'm not saying cut off your relationships or blow off other people. That's avoidance. 'No man is an island' John Donne wisely pointed out. Your focus is simply to reduce your own attachment blockage so that you can feel confident in making decisions on your own, in doing things you want to do, regardless of whether someone is there alongside you to support you. It is about becoming healthy, not about becoming indifferent to others. And as you grow kinder and more accepting of yourself, you will find yourself viewing others in a kindlier light. You might be surprised at how many people become inspired by the changes they see in you and start modelling themselves after you.

Establish healthy boundaries

Having boundaries keeps you on track, especially when you are tired and fatigued. Not establishing boundaries is a bit like trying to diet without having given any thought or effort into preparing your meals and having no idea how many calories you consume. Instead, you just eat the same things and convince yourself that somehow the outcome will be different. It won't.

However, if you are prepared, when you have given thought as to what you will do when facing various situations, you are far more likely to stay on track. Much like a diet program, you can simply heat up a dish, even when you are tired. You do not worry about exceeding your calorie count, etc. because it has all been calculated. You know what and how to do it, because you have set boundaries.

Surround yourself with the right people. Align yourself with people who are confident in their actions and do not need to rely on others' approval before moving forward. They will inspire you to do the same. People who are self-reliant are not threatened by others, and have no unhealthy desire to sabotage anyone. Instead, they welcome having other people to step up and challenge themselves. They know how great it feels and they want everyone to share that experience.

SUMMARY

- Our first exposure to a relationship is via our primary caregiver, who is most often our mother. How this relationship evolves has a large bearing on our confidence as a child.

- When a child senses it cannot continuously rely on its caregiver for support, it compensates in other ways, such as transference to a security object, or by withdrawing/camouflaging its need by feigning indifference.

- The more you learn about your attachment blockage, the more you can influence and overcome it. By working on your attachment blockage step by step, you empower yourself to slowly but surely make progress.

- In a balanced relationship, control and responsibility are aligned. Alignment occurs where a person takes responsibility over something that is within their control and relinquish responsibility over the things that are not within their control.

- When we recognise and accept our attachment blockage, we can start to be kind to ourselves and take steps to overcome it. Instead of blaming everyone else, we take responsibility for our own actions. Self-acceptance means we do not blame others for how we feel, and we can forgive ourselves and others more readily.

Blockage 2: The Emptiness Blockage

> *Acknowledging the good that you already have in your life is the foundation for all abundance.*
>
> — Eckhart Tolle

Have you noticed that some people ridicule others consistently for no apparent reason? Have you ever wondered why some persons with demanding, often highly paid careers, with little time for anything else, express contempt for those who settle down and start a family? Conversely, you may know people who, lacking financial success themselves, attribute the financial success of others as 'mere luck'. Further, they might describe wealthy people as ruthless or selfish.

People with an emptiness blockage exhibit what is called denial, an unconscious process that prevents us from facing or admitting to things that make us uncomfortable or we find painful. People who are scared or uncomfortable confronting what is missing in their own lives often criticise others who have what they don't. This is particularly the case if they see other people who seem happy with the choices they've made. They deny the painful feelings and thoughts that arise from awareness of the life experiences they are missing out on.

The emptiness blockage often develops as a result of childhood stuckburies. Parents harbouring strong ambitions for their children, and who show a preference for activities they want their children to be involved in, may reward their children's efforts in those activities whilst exhibiting indifference or outright disapproval of activities they do not value.

Accordingly, those children focus their energies on the areas they know they will be rewarded for, striving hard to become skilled at these activities, whilst often abandoning activities for which approval is rare or impossible to come by, no matter how much they enjoy them.

This behaviour continues into adulthood, with continued emphasis on what they have worked hard to master, and neglecting whatever their parents dismissed as worthless or unimportant. Things like physical affection, consideration of others, and sportsmanlike behaviour are just a few examples of things that can get pushed aside.

Underlying the emptiness blockage is the unconscious wish for the approval of their parents. The parents of children who develop the emptiness blockage later in life can be focused and driven themselves, honing their skills at whatever they are good at, whilst ignoring other important things. This provides a model for the children to emulate as they grow to become adults.

Living example of an emptiness blockage

Dimitri, at six years old, loved drawing and music. His parents ran a successful family business in logistics, which had been in existence for over 120 years.

Dimitri went virtually everywhere with his parents, even to the occasional board meeting if a babysitter was not available. He drew extensively, excitedly showing his drawings to his parents. His parents would glance at them, shake their heads with a smile, and say, 'That's nice, Dimitri, but remember that one day you will be managing the family business with your brothers and there won't be time for such things.' This, they assured him, was their legacy to him and that he should be grateful that he had a successful future ahead of him.

As he grew, his parents pressured him to excel in maths, as that would help him with the family business later on. They were frequently busy and preoccupied with work when they got home, but they always made a big fuss over him when he achieved excellent maths grades. Dimitri's future was mapped out and he worked hard to please his parents, revelling in the attention it brought him.

As an adult, Dimitri worked his way up and began running the company when his parents retired. He often worked up to 18 hours a day, rarely seeing his wife and children. The more Dimitri worked, the more he felt something was missing. The company was doing well, he was a success by anyone's standards, yet he felt disenchanted with his life and disconnected from his family.

Do you feel like your life is lacking in some ways but you can't put your finger on what would create that elusive sense of wholeness? You may suffer from an emptiness blockage if you purposefully limit your focus to just one or two goals and hold yourself back from performing to your full potential. When you focus just on just work, for example, in order to achieve a sense of fulfilment, you neglect other important aspects, leaving you feeling empty, with a life that lacks purpose or meaning.

We all have needs, things that make us feel secure and happy. People with the emptiness blockage deny to themselves the importance of their needs.

The reason for the deep feeling of emptiness stems from a more holistic purpose or goal in life. According to Maslow's Hierarchy of Needs theory, people are motivated to achieve certain needs, starting with the most basic biological/physiological needs to ensure survival (food, water, shelter, sleep, etc.) and next up to safety (security, stability), and then, when all of those are met, belongingness and love (affection, relationships), esteem (achievement, status, reputation) and, ultimately, self-actualisation (personal growth and fulfilment).

Dimitri, in his quest for success and resulting feelings of disconnection from his family, is stuck on level two. He has achieved security and stability but cannot get past his focus on that to work on belongingness and love.

Our goal in achieving true success in our lives is to progress up the levels of need to eventually focus on and attain self-actualisation. It is a bit like learning to ski – if you get better and better at what you do but never let yourself leave the intermediate slope for the advanced (never mind the expert slope), no matter how accomplished you are on that intermediate slope, after a while, skiing becomes boring and unfulfilling. Dimitri has spent his entire working life on the intermediate slope but has never risked seeing what challenges the advanced slope holds.

People who experience this feeling of emptiness but stay within their familiar sphere, channel their need for more into getting more of what they already have instead of what they don't have. They do not know what else to do to make themselves happy because they were taught that what they do is the end goal, the most important thing. They continue to bury themselves in what they see is their role in life, driven by their denial of what else is lacking in their life. In essence, fear dominates their personality to such a degree that they cannot function outside the realm of their emptiness blockage.

Understanding why you feel empty is the first step to resolving an emptiness blockage. Identifying the stuckburies, the causes for an emptiness blockage, as with any blockage, can be difficult, and mere recognition of it is not enough to resolve the blockage; it requires vigorous action to resolve it. However, in resolving the blockage, you will notice much improvement in your life.

Free association

We touched upon free association as it is used in psychotherapy in the 'Stuckburies' section at the start of the book. Practising free association, allowing your thoughts to come freely, can help you to get to the source of your problems. You can improve your life by learning things about yourself, things that you have not been aware of and that you had not ever experienced in yourself. The emptiness blockage previously allowed you to avoid these aspects.

Values

Taking time out to think about what matters to you, what your values are, and then engaging in activities that align with those values, will make you feel happy and fulfilled. This does not just apply to selfless acts and charitable works. If your work life is demanding but you've always wistfully thought how nice it would be to garden, stop waiting and do it! Get out there and get your hands dirty. If you'd like to be closer to your family, start by finding out what things you all like to do, whether it is hiking, movie night, or going to an amusement park, and make it happen. Make it a regular occurrence, whether it is weekly, monthly, or whatever. Applying your values and principles to your life will imbue a greater sense of purpose and meaning to your life.

People with the emptiness blockage often do not take time out to realise the bigger picture. They get caught up in being critical, jealous, or just plain unhappy and never take a deep breath and examine what the big picture is.

If they fast-forwarded 50 years, they would likely find themselves regretting everything they did not do. By looking at the big picture, you look at what lies ahead. Do you like what you see? If not, then be proactive in finding ways to change that.

Defining success

In looking at the big picture, total success is the filter through which you view it. Our definition of our individual success typically relates to whether we achieve our long-term plans. If your definition of success is owning 10 properties, but your values include being a great dad, then you have some adjustments to make. (Principle 1 takes a closer look at achieving true success.)

When you start to believe in yourself, you begin to tap into your hidden potential. But how on earth do you start to believe in yourself if you've never learned to do so? The key may lie in looking back and recognising the achievements you've made that were never previously acknowledged.

Think back to when you challenged yourself. Maybe as a child you conquered your fear and climbed a tree that seemed impossible. What about when you first learned to ride a bike? How did that completely unfamiliar feeling of freedom strike you then?

Remember when you learned to drive a car? Particularly if you learned to drive a standard versus an automatic, there was so much to remember, so much at stake. You had to juggle your handling of an unfamiliar piece of equipment not just with your hands but with your feet whilst staying between the lines and not hitting anything. What about the first time you took the car out onto the highway? That was definitely scary. But you did it, didn't you?

When did you lose your sense of wonder and adventure, your willingness to take a chance?

Take a moment now to think back to when you did something that scared you, something you may have been convinced you couldn't do but you managed to do it anyway, if not the first time, then when you persisted. How did it make you feel?

Don't worry about where you feel you may have failed. Failures are merely steps towards success, as long as you do not give in to fear, as long as you do not stop moving forward. Did you ever skate as a kid? Strapping on those skates was exciting, partly because of the risk of falling, but mainly because of the adrenalin rush when you got good enough that you didn't fall.

Do not worry about comparing yourself to others. This is your journey, not theirs; they've got their own path to worry about. Keep your eyes fixed firmly forward and take that next step, and reward yourself in some way for every achievement.

Take the '1010 Challenge'

Belief in ourselves gives us confidence to try new things. If we believe hard enough, we have the potential to achieve greatness.

Pick 10 things you have always wanted to achieve but have not. Maybe you've tried but have not done them yet or maybe you've never tried. Write them down. Now, under each goal, write down 10 activities that will start you on your way to achieving each goals. Visualise it. For example, if you've always wanted to dance but feel you have two left feet, you could start by watching some aerobic exercise videos and learning the steps. Then you can try line dancing (which incorporates many of the steps of aerobics without as much exertion), neither of which requires a partner. Now, what else could you do once you have learned a few dances and feel better about knowing your right from your left? Group classes are often available, as are private lessons. Work your way up to feeling comfortable trying out your steps at a community dance perhaps. Think of 10 things you can do to get yourself dancing.

One of my goals was travelling to Africa to see 'The Big 5'. The Big 5 are the five top safari animals, but the real reason this was a struggle for me is because I'm claustrophobic. I'd never flown anywhere before. Just the thought of being on a plane from Melbourne to Africa for 30 hours had me sweating profusely. I overcame it by focusing on the feeling of excitement I would have in seeing all the animals I had only dreamed of seeing, ever since I was a child. (I also took my laptop on the plane, because although I know I ideally should not be working on a holiday, work was the only thing I could think of that could significantly distract me from feeling claustrophobic.) The result? I did it! And I have been able to fly without undue anxiety ever since.

Inspirational speaker Tony Robbins notes that what we can or cannot do, or consider possible, is usually related to what we believe about ourselves, rather than our true capability. If you think you can, you can. If you think you can't, then you'll be right about that too. It is your choice.

It's not about doing *the* best; it's about doing *your* best

If you've always wanted to try rock climbing, the odds are you are not going to start out by trying to scale Mount Everest. What we are talking about here is trying something achievable and doing it to the best of your ability, no matter where that ability level measures. If you try to achieve something and don't get there, but you know that you have done your best and that realistically you are not going to be able to do more, there will still be a great sense of satisfaction in having tried, and certainly no lingering regrets for never having tried. When you struggle with an emptiness blockage, taking a risk and doing your best at something new and unfamiliar is particularly challenging. But it is also the way to overcome your emptiness blockage.

Balance is the key here. The only way you are going to feel down is if you judge yourself with guilt. By trying too hard or not enough, we risk losing our joy in life, and that is not healthy. Immersing yourself in something is great, yes, and it can make you intuitive, but you also need to have the joys. By reducing the emptiness, we can try to do things that we might otherwise feel are impossible. The level of effort needs to be balanced though, so we do not compromise life and feel lethargic.

Internal incentives

Emptiness blockage intensifies when we are alone. The room seems emptier, whereas being proactive and taking action, doing new things and taking little risks, energises us. Simultaneously, it stops us ridiculing others whom we are jealous of. We become the people we were secretly admiring but publicly insulting. We can turn that around to respect ourselves and publicly show our magnificence by trying to step up.

The problem is that most people need an incentive to do things. When we do things that can better us, we do not appreciate the reward. For example, working extra hours and getting a bonus may be worth more to you than getting on a crowded bus for the first time in 10 years because you suffer from anxiety. You may fail to appreciate the true value in doing the mental work to get your mind right before getting on a bus.

When you do your best, you take risks. The most amazing thing about it is that you do not have any regrets. You do not wake up cursing the fact that your neighbour has managed to buy a new car, because you are excited about what you started yesterday, or what you are about to attempt with your life. You do not have to please anyone; you just step up and do your best, because you know it will start to clear the blockages that developed way back when your stuckbury first formed.

As you begin to reduce your emptiness blockage and see more clearly how you have acted in the past, you may find yourself feeling guilty about how you've treated or acted around others. Remorse is fine if it is incentive to improve and repair relationships. Just do not let it paralyse you and prevent you from moving forward. When you let go of the past, you give yourself the opportunity to be fully awake and alive to life. Accept that you will have muck-ups and slip back into your old ways, but do not sit there feeling guilty about it – do something. Allow yourself to slip, and allow yourself to get up.

When you let go of the past, you can focus on the future. Every day is new. You no longer have the emptiness blockage that keeps you doing the same thing every day, with the same negative attitude. Each day will bring surprises.

SUMMARY

- In our minds, we use denial as a defence mechanism, an unconscious strategy to avoid acknowledging the truth because of the pain it can bring.

- Investing in only one facet of life, such as work, at the expense of others, stems from an emptiness blockage.

- Those suffering an emptiness blockage feel dissatisfied because they are not addressing all their needs.

- We have the power to change those beliefs that do not help us to move forward.

- Understanding the reasons that underlie feelings of emptiness is the first step to resolving an emptiness blockage.

- Identifying your values and principles – what matters most to you – and engaging in activities that promote those values will leave you feeling happier and more fulfilled. It gives a sense of purpose and meaning to life.

Blockage 3: The Intellectual Blockage

> *All learning has an emotional base.*
>
> Plato

Have you ever had a bad day at work that you replayed over and over again in your mind to the point where it made you dread the idea of returning the next day?

Have you ever looked forward to an event with anticipation but, as the event nears, you find yourself fielding anxious thoughts about what might go wrong to ruin it? And, by the time it's time to go, you are dreading going instead of being excited. By now, you've convinced yourself that going is not a good idea.

Emotions colour our perception of our world. When we feel negative, the world around us is not inviting. When we feel positive, the world brims with possibilities. In reality, the world is the world – the only thing that changes is how we choose to perceive it.

Living example of an intellectual blockage

Simone had been unemployed for six months. She went for three job interviews and two went well. Company A's job offered a higher salary and was conveniently close to home. Company B was offering considerably less money and was located further away, but they were more eager to hire her and asked if she could start the following week. Simone was torn. She wanted the better-paying job with the easier commute but Company A did not offer her the job right away. Instead, they said they would let her know about the job in 24 to 48 hours.

After 24 hours, when she had not heard anything, she phoned and left a message. An hour later, she phoned again and left another message. She began feeling anxious and replayed the interview in her head over and over again. What could she do, she wondered, to convince them she was the right person for the job? Company B, on the other hand, was pressing her for a decision.

That night she tossed and turned, uncertain what to do. What if Company A didn't offer her the job? What if she had to take the job at Company B and didn't like it and was now saddled with a much lower salary and nearly twice the commute? The next day she woke up tired and distressed. She phoned Company A multiple times, each time leaving a message. She insisted to the receptionist that it was urgent that the personnel manager return her call as soon as possible.

After more than 48 hours, with still no word from Company A, and fearful of finding herself without either job, she phoned Company B and accepted the job. The following day, Company A called. She began babbling that she'd accepted another position but that she would turn it down. She hurried off the phone before the personnel manager could change her mind and called Company B to tell them she would not be taking the job after all. The manager sounded annoyed with her and she began to make excuses. The call did not end well.

Despite having been offered the job she wanted, Simone felt anxious about calling them. She wondered whether she had made the right decision. Company B had clearly been more enthusiastic about hiring her. She rang the personnel manager at Company A and felt flustered when the receptionist said the manager was busy. She left a message insisting the manager call her back immediately. She called again in an hour and left another message. She did the same an hour later.

By the time Company A's manager called her back, she was practically in a full-blown panic. The manager sensed her hysteria and, not wanting to hire a potentially unstable employee, promptly apologised for any confusion and said the position had already been filled. A frantic call back to Company B yielded the same result – there was no job for Simone.

Because Simone had let her feelings of desperation and anxiety cloud her perception, she ended up missing out on both jobs.

When we are stuck in the intellectual block, we over-think things. We fear so much that our emotion is magnified and we act in haste, whether it is quitting a job, a relationship, or missing out on an opportunity.

As a child, you may have felt insecure in your parents' attention. Perhaps your caregiver was inconsistent in their behaviour. That uncertainty and instability may have taught us to over-analyse things to the point where our insecurities push people away.

A colleague of mine was once sitting next to me during a presentation. The room had seating for only 30 people but there were at least 50 of us, with people lining the walls. He began to sweat and fidget. When I asked him what was wrong, he said he felt cramped and trapped. He'd recently put on a bit of weight and his clothes felt too tight and restrictive. The feeling got so bad that he hastily got up and left.

He did not have to run out. He could have stood at the back of the room. At the time, however, rationale went out the window and panic and fear set in.

There are other ways people use to handle this kind of stress building up inside. Some people scratch or bite their nails until they bleed. Someone might punch a wall to vent their pent-up fears. Some indulge in binge eating or abuse alcohol or caffeine, anti-anxiety tablets, or drugs in general to numb the pain. These are distractions, not solutions, and harmful ones at that. By running away every time these feelings occur, you create a learnt behaviour. You learn to run away at the slightest sign of stress. When this happens, you feel negative emotions associated with the negative behaviours, like feeling guilty or disappointed in yourself. Once you create a disturbing image of yourself at work, it can become difficult for you.

If you continually run away, you never learn healthy ways to cope with these emotions. And, as you get older, the handling methods may become more extreme. Health issues can arise.

This is not about eliminating all negative emotions. Feelings of fear can alert us to real danger and help keep us safe. The point here is to distinguish between healthy fear and unhealthy fear.

When over-thinking an idea or issue, we question our motives and look for flaws. When trying to make a decision, we focus too much on what could go wrong. We look at alternatives to determine if a different option could produce a better result. The more we think something through, the more issues and problems may arise as a result. It is less likely that we will decide to go ahead.

We begin to ignore the benefits of progress, and the fear outweighs any possible benefits. The decision-making process breaks down. Fearful of what could go wrong, we cannot act. The intellectual block is driven by our fears that we are not up to the task and we are not adequately prepared.

Eckhart Tolle theorised that one of the most common yet least talked about addictions is thinking. In one of his talks, 'How do we break the habit of excessive thinking?' he refers to the act of thinking as being addictive, like smoking, drinking, or eating. Thinking can move from one thought into a series of thoughts, before escalating into a veritable horror story if we let our fears run rampant.

Implicit and explicit thinking

There are two types of memory, implicit and explicit. *Explicit memory* is conscious and coherent. If a task is completed using explicit memory processes, you are consciously thinking about the task whilst you are completing it. (This is often referred to as mindful thinking.) For example, if you are driving someplace you've never been to before, you are paying attention to what you are doing, to road signs, landmarks, and anything else that can help you find your way to your destination.

Implicit memory is unconscious, harder to define, and intuitive. When you use implicit memory processes to complete a task, you are doing something without thinking about it. For example, if you are driving a route that you travel every day, your mind may wander to other things and your actual driving is being done on mental autopilot. Breathing and walking are two more examples of tasks we perform without giving them the slightest thought, unless they cannot be done without difficulty.

Scientists have determined that processes associated with one memory type can interfere with the processes of the other memory type. When research participants handled an implicit task in a conscious and explicit way, performance was more self-conscious, not as effortless, impairing the performance of the task.

The same can be said for the natural flow of creativity. In one study, participants had their brain activity monitored when asked to draw a picture based on a verbal description (e.g., 'Draw a flower'). Those whose drawings scored high in creativity corresponded with individuals whose brain activity centred on motor control rather than conscious thinking and effort. Creativity flows more freely when we do not try so hard. Manish Saggar, a psychiatrist at Stanford, summarised this as 'the more you think about it, the more you mess it up.'

Mindfulness – living in the moment

When you are constantly thinking, worrying and analysing, you are not in the moment. You are thinking about either the past or the future. You do not have any control. Where can you go from these thoughts? Rather than worrying about what went wrong in the past, or what could go wrong in the future, concentrate on what you can do *in this present moment.*

In today's society, there is an emphasis upon rationality and evidence-based decision-making. At school, we are taught to think things through, to plan, and to revise what could go wrong. This thinking is evident in our education system, our legal system, and our medical system. From an early age, it is ingrained into us that if we operate 'by the seat of our pants' or 'without structure', we will invariably fail.

We are taught to focus upon ensuring that nothing can go wrong, rather than thinking of the things that can happen for us. If you look only at the negative, you will be unable to see the positive, and vice versa.

Successful entrepreneurs develop idea-based growth strategies. For example, Richard Branson, founder of Virgin Group, many years ago envisaged flying passengers into space, to orbit around the Earth. Back then, this idea sounded like something from a science fiction novel, yet Richard Branson was undeterred and has made it a reality.

Richard Branson created much of his empire by listening to his intuition, and following his spirit for adventure. People who are not intellectually blocked make decisions quickly and are dedicated to developing their ideas. They are reluctant to abandon their ideas, even in the face of obstacles.

Blockage triggers

Once you recognise that you have an intellectual blockage, the first step is to analyse how it affects you. What kinds of situations trigger over-thinking in you? Is it fear of losing or not finding a job? How to resolve conflicts between yourself and others? Is it the prospect of certain social situations? Maybe it is just stepping outside your front door. Whatever it is, see it merely as an identifier – this is not about beating yourself up over your perceived inadequacies.

If you are not sure what your triggers are, think back to the last time you used a negative coping strategy, such as comfort or binge eating when you feel nervous or uncomfortable, reaching for alcohol or pills, or simply working yourself up into a nervous lather. What was it that caused you to indulge in harmful behaviour? Maybe you went out and got drunk after an argument with your partner. If so, it may be that relationship issues are a trigger for you. Perhaps you bit your nails until they bled after your boss would not take your repeated calls. That trigger would be a work-related control issue.

Signals

Once you become more conscious of your triggers, you become more aware of the various signals your body gives off before using a negative coping mechanism. Signals can include heightened emotions, agitation, guilt, or fear, for example. You may have destructive reactions, saying to yourself, 'My life is terrible', 'I'm not strong enough', or 'There is no way out'. Other signals could be slumping, twitching, feeling your energy levels spike or plummet, changes in your behaviour, such as becoming erratic, yelling, refusing to eat or overeating, and demanding reassurance from others.

The following table is designed to help you analyse what may trigger an intellectual blockage and how to identify the signals, the various negative coping mechanisms you typically resort to (e.g., stress-induced eating). Using the example below as a guideline, take a few moments to identify some triggers in your life and how they manifest in terms of your behaviour.

Trigger	*When my spouse threatens me with ultimatums*
Warning signal	*I feel cornered, coerced, manipulated*
Thoughts	*I can't live like this anymore.* *I may need to separate.* *It's hurting my career. It's affecting my weight.* *I hate my life.*
Physical reaction	*Twitching, sweating, dry lips, nail biting, short temper, low concentration*
Negative coping mechanism	*Pacing, binge-eating chocolate, nervously drumming table, coughing, drinking alcohol*

Now that you've identified some of the primary triggers that push you into an intellectual blockage and what behaviours you exhibited when faced with those triggers, let's look at some examples of steps you can put into practise to help you to more constructively confront these behaviours, cope with stressful situations, and resolve your anxiety.

Techniques to overcome anxiety	*This is just a thought; it will pass.* *Things aren't what they seem.* *Stop doing what isn't helping.* *Focus on the good things in life.*
Results	*Appreciation/gratitude for being fit and healthy and a good person.* *Telling myself that this will pass only puts me under more pressure. I need a more active strategy, like going for a run, going to the gym, training sessions with my dog, working in the garden...*
Commitment	*I will commit to practising more appreciation/gratitude, because when I do, my twitching ceases and I feel calmer, more relaxed. When I find myself reaching for chocolate, I'll drink water instead. When my spouse gives me the silent treatment, I will give them space to cool down before approaching them again.*

Being more aware of your intellectual block gives you the freedom to choose to react differently. If you know you are obsessive about people calling back, commit to ringing them only once or twice. Listen to relaxing music or do something physical until the urge subsides. Try journaling. Keep trying new things until you hit on ones that work, ones that you can make into new habits.

Be patient with yourself

It is easy to become impatient once you've identified your blockage and its triggers. But changing habits, behaviours learnt over the course of a lifetime, takes time. It can be helpful to document your progress, listing what elements you try that help you cope more constructively, how their consistent application improves your reactions to trigger situations, and ultimately documenting when you've succeeded in breaking those old habits and leaving your intellectual blockage behind.

Let's look at what this progression might look like in someone who has control issues.

Trigger:	Your client hasn't called you back as promised.
Negative coping mechanism:	You repeatedly telephone your client, perhaps as often as every hour or every half hour, until you can get them on the phone.
Initial behavioural goal:	Pledge not to call your client more than once or twice a day.
Improvement:	You are not obsessing so much about the client not phoning. You feel capable of turning your attention to other things that need doing and only giving this your attention for a small part of your day versus worrying excessively.

Success: When your client fails to call regarding a potential sale and you could use the sale to boost your numbers, you are still willing to avoid phoning them more than once a day to prod them, and are comfortable turning your attention towards other clients and things that need attention without obsessing over this.

If you find yourself unable to stop over-thinking, focus on the present, starting with your breathing. Listen to how frequent your breaths are, how shallow or deep they are, how your chest feels when you inhale and exhale. Paying attention to your surroundings and your body interrupts excessive thinking and helps to re-calibrate your mind. Being in the present resets your thoughts, relaxing you and enabling you to make better decisions because you are now in a calmer state of mind.

Risk and success

Risk and success go hand in hand. You cannot push beyond your limits to succeed without taking risks. Success does not lie in playing it safe, staying within your comfort zone. We are not talking about being reckless here, but if, intuitively, it feels right, then do it. Failures are rarely as damaging or permanent as we fear. Fix problems as they arise and adopt the attitude of 'Why not go for it, and see what happens?'

Let's consider Tony, who owns a business that has been successful in the past but is feeling frustrated because it has been stagnant for several years. He does not understand internet marketing, social media, or lease agreements. Tony would prefer simply to work in his shop as he always has. He is terrified of debt and change, and generally scared to expand his business, even though he knows that his business will continue to fall behind the competition.

Tony needs to team up with someone who does not share his intellectual blockage and is eager to try new things. Naturally, different styles can breed conflict but if they learn how to handle their conflicts constructively and his new partner can demonstrate how new approaches and strategies can improve the business, Tony can feel more comfortable taking that leap and trying something new. Ironically, the person best situated to help you overcome such a blockage is usually the person you find yourself in conflict with. As long as the conflicts are not destructive but instead are breeding grounds for negotiation and experimentation, you will make progress. This is true for both business and personal relationships.

Baby steps

The first step to resolving an intellectual blockage is to start *small*. Take lots of little risks so that when you make a mistake, you can fix it. Do something different daily. If talking to strangers is difficult for you, make a point of smiling or greeting one new person each day. Perform a random act of kindness for a stranger. Keep adding new things each week until you have diversified your life into a new, broader, and more creative direction. Over time you will develop the confidence to take even bigger risks.

SUMMARY

- Over-thinking stems from fear and magnifies our emotional responses. By over-analysing, you risk getting stuck in place instead of moving forward.

- Thinking about things too much can inhibit your ability to do activities that otherwise come naturally.

- Thinking can be just as addictive as smoking, drinking, and eating. Over-thinking is an unhealthy habit that prevents you from progressing in life.

- Slow and steady wins the race – take small steps and steadily increase them.

- Being in the present stops you from over-thinking. Simple activities such as breathing or paying attention to your surroundings interrupt excessive thinking and reset and relax your mind.

Blockage 4: The Depression Blockage

> *Change will not come if we wait for some other person or some other time. We are the ones we've been waiting for. We are the change that we seek.*
>
> — Barack Obama

These days, be it on television, in the newspaper, on the internet, and even on social media, more and more advertisements appear from mental health organisations and pharmaceutical corporations that offer ways to overcome depression. Are all these people depressed? Or are they simply suppressing their stuckburies and need a little help?

How do we know if someone is depressed? Common signs can include feeling blue or miserable for extended periods of time, and struggling to function day to day, starting with getting out of bed in the morning. People with depressive block believe something is wrong with the way they feel and how their brain functions. They feel the only way to relieve their suffering is to take medication. They feel helpless and trapped, convinced they cannot change how they feel.

The statistics on depression are, in themselves, depressing. Globally, about 350 million people suffer from depression.[11] About 800,000 Australians experience depression annually, and, on average, one in both four women and six men will suffer from depression at some point.[12] Many celebrities, the Mental Health Research Institute says, including Garry McDonald,

Natalie Bassingthwaighte, and Rachel Griffiths, have shared their experience with depression to reduce stigma about the illness.

As more accurate information has become available, the illness has gradually begun losing its stigma. However, instead of seeking early medical intervention, many people are self-diagnosing, which can often unnecessarily prolong their suffering. If we broaden our understanding of depression, we can better address the root causes, or stuckburies, that form the underlying blockages that often result in depression.

Feeling depressed

The word 'depressed' is commonly associated with feeling down. It is important to distinguish between the occasional sadness we feel, which is perfectly normal, and actual deep-rooted depression. Clinical depression can be serious and long term, generating feelings of tiredness, hopelessness, irritability, physical and mental slowness, and differences in sleeping and eating habits, impairing your ability to function normally. With no end to the despair in sight, it can drive someone to the extreme in order to end the suffering, to the point where he/she may take his or her own life.

Just because you experience periodic bouts of feeling blue does not mean you suffer from depression. The depression blockage occurs when you feel unable to fulfil your dreams and aspirations because you are convinced that you suffer from clinical depression, when in fact you do not. Everyone experiences feelings of sadness, ineffectiveness, lethargy, and such, and they do pass. You may just be in a low place and time of your life. Some people are regrettably diagnosed as suffering from depression when it is simply a depression blockage, something that can be worked through and resolved.

In a majority of people, depression can be linked to a combination of chemical, psychological, and general living factors. Early childhood experiences, including stuckbury development, can occur as a result of poor parenting, bullying, or one or more traumatic events, for example. Having a serious traumatic experience when just a child can lead someone to foster negative beliefs about themselves and certain life situations.

Living example of a depression blockage

Joanna was a supervisor at a large company and loved her job. The company went into financial crisis and laid off a number of its employees. Joanna was one of them.

Joanna was devastated. Although she knew she had not been the only one let go, she felt ashamed, somehow convinced that she was responsible for having lost her job. It brought back vivid memories of how, as a quiet child who had been a bit smaller than her peers, she'd been bullied in school. She had not spoken of it at home, convinced then as well that it had somehow been her fault, that she had done something to deserve all the humiliating treatment she'd been subjected to. She became more and more withdrawn, not wanting to look for another job, not even wanting to talk to friends and family. Her family were worried about her. Claiming fatigue, she spent days in bed.

Two months after she'd been laid off, she was still spending more time in bed than out, and her energy levels were low. When she did get out of bed, she would drink several bottles of wine and stumble back to bed, intent on escaping her pervasive feelings of shame and failure. Joanna was not suffering from clinical depression. Instead, she was stuck in the depression blockage, her intense reaction to losing her job stemming from the traumatic bullying she'd received at school.

Depression blockage stems from a fear-based emotion from the past. When certain events happen, these 'triggers' can launch the emotions associated with the painful past event(s) and intense feelings of sadness and inability to cope surface. Everything seems more overwhelming than it is and the instinct can be to hide, to bury yourself away from life, which you associate with the pain.

If you suffer from bouts of depression, it is important to uncover the source of it, and that means seeing a professional. If your depression is the result of a chemical imbalance, a doctor can help you with that. If your depression derives from a painful incident in your past, a therapist can help you uncover what it is and identify new coping mechanisms for you to try. If you suffer from a stuckbury, it may require you to risk doing something you believe you can't do in order to overcome it.

It is important to note that you could in fact be suffering from depression as well as from a depression blockage caused by a stuckbury. But for many, a blockage may prevent us from realising our true potential and doing what is necessary to be successful. If something affects us in a way that generates the same feelings that we felt when we suffered a painful childhood experience, we can either give in to those feelings and allow ourselves to sink into depression or we can try to do something to resolve it once and for all, by controlling our thoughts and finding more constructive ways of dealing with situations. You are not helpless. But depression blockage can convince you that you are helpless.

Living example of a depression blockage

Jerry has been depressed on and off for most of his life and has been taking medication for the past 20 years. He finds it difficult to work and prefers jobs that offer quiet graveyard shifts where he does not have to interact with many people. He finds dealing with people challenging and often engages in self-sabotaging behaviours, turning up late for work and being hostile and uncooperative towards his colleagues. He has never held any job for long.

Jerry's parents are comfortably off and can assist Jerry financially, which enables his behaviour. Because he can afford to remain unemployed, he has not bothered to address any of the underlying causes. The situation is compounded by Jerry's reliance on medication to manage his condition. Taking pills is a lot easier than making the effort to improve his depression with lifestyle changes such as exercise and keeping normal hours. Instead, Jerry uses his illness as an excuse not to take proactive action. Jerry has the depression blockage.

Walking

Walking briskly is arguably one of the best remedies for mood elevation. When you walk or do any exercise, you focus outward rather than inward. Look around you, smile at people, feel the energy, the air blowing. Vigorous exercise of any kind gets endorphins flowing, those hormones in your body that suppress pain and promote feelings of euphoria. Scientists have discovered that the positive effects of exercise on depressed patients last longer than those of anti-depressants.

A study published in a Harvard Medical School report in 2005 found that walking at an accelerated pace for 35 minutes a day, five times a week, or for one hour a day, three times a week, had a significant influence on mild to moderate depression symptoms.[13] Walking fast for only 15 minutes a day, five times a week, or doing stretching exercises three times a week, it was noted, did not help as much.

The next time you feel low, stop for a moment and rank your mood, zero being the lowest you've ever felt, and 10 being happiest. Now, go for a brisk half-hour walk. The minute you stop, rank how you feel. Sense any difference? Most likely, you will feel markedly better. This is an excellent reminder that you have the ability to improve your mood yourself, without medication – you are not impossibly stuck.

A way to address the depression blockage is to stop the negative vortex that spirals you into a whirlwind of despair and helplessness.

When you find something like a favourite form of exercise that can stop you from plummeting into negativity and despair, that's a great step forward in the healing process. Even taking a shower can help.

Keep a list of, and grade, the activities that work best for you and note how long your improved mood lasts. Avoid things like sugar highs, which can give you a brief boost but are artificial – not only do they not last but they are unhealthy.

The switch strategy

The next time you start feeling down and thinking destructive thoughts for at least 15 minutes, think of one thing that you are grateful for in your life and focus on it. Why are you grateful for it? What has it added to your life? Start keeping a 'gratitude and appreciation' list to remind yourself of all the good things going on in your life. This is a great practice because it not only forces you to focus on how long you might be indulging in negative thoughts but also helps you to reorient your perspective and think about positive things instead.

It might be helpful for you to keep track of when this happens, how long you've let yourself indulge in negative thoughts, what positive aspect you consciously chose to switch your attention to, and how well it worked, if you are not sure how effective this strategy is for you.

Let's take a look at what such a page might look like for someone who's anxious about being unemployed. It may also prove helpful to keep track of the days that you do this, as you may find the gaps between when you feel depressed start to widen. You may not even realise how you need to do this less and less frequently until you compare the dates.

The Switch Strategy Table

Date	Depressive thought	Time spent feeling depressed	Gratitude/ appreciation replacement thought	Effectiveness scale (0 to 10)
	How will I pay my rent if I can't find a job?	25 minutes	I'm grateful I've been able to save enough money to cover me for a couple of months.	3 – I don't want to use my savings but what if I can't find a job?
	I still don't have a job.	15 minutes	I've got some promising leads and a couple pay more money than my last job so I might be better off now.	9 – I took a walk when focusing on this and I felt inspired to get to the next level in my career.
	I've put on a lot of weight recently because I've been eating more junk food. I don't like the way I look or feel.	12 minutes	I have plenty of opportunity to exercise now that I'm between jobs, which means I can lose the weight more quickly if I stop binging.	6 – This gives me something positive to focus on whilst I'm not working and I'll look better than ever when I do get a job!

Faulty connections

Before fixing an electrical problem in your house, you first need to identify whether there are any faulty connections. The same can be said of the healing process for being stuck in the depression blockage. We sometimes make the wrong connection. For example, do we forecast the worst possible outcome before a situation happens? And, if so, how often does the worst-case scenario happen? Are we, perhaps, willing it to happen?

Shakespeare famously wrote, 'There is nothing either good or bad, but thinking makes it so.'

Scenario: Mike finds himself coughing one day and convinces himself that he's getting pneumonia. He promptly goes down to the chemist and buys $40 worth of over-the-counter medications. When he wakes up the next morning feeling markedly better, instead of feeling relieved and happy by this, he berates himself by thinking, *I'm a total idiot. I thought I would get pneumonia and threw away a lot of money I can't afford to waste. I'm so stupid. My parents were right. My brother's so much smarter than me. He would never be this stupid...*

By thinking the worst about his cough, Mike exaggerated the severity of his getting sick, and when it didn't happen, instead of being relieved he is angry at himself. He compares himself to his more successful brother and gets even more upset by how inferior he's convinced he is. This downward spiral comes from Mike's thoughts, not from what's happening. When we catch ourselves in this downward thought spiral, we can choose to think other, more uplifting thoughts, which has a direct effect on our mood.

In the example of the preceding table, where someone has lost their job and is feeling anxious about finding another one in time to be able to pay the rent without dipping into precious savings, let's take a look at how this person is capable of steering his or her thoughts in a more positive direction.

Situation: *I've lost my job, and now I'm under tremendous financial strain.*

Depressive train of thought: *I'm hopeless. I'll be unemployed forever. The economy is so bad. The situation is hopeless. My entire life is hopeless. What's the point? I'm depressed and it's ruining my life.*

Mindset: *I'm a victim.*

More positive train of thought: *Unemployment is on the rise. I'm not alone – it's affecting a lot of people. I've got marketable skills. I might even find a better job now, maybe even a better career track.*

Resulting mindset: *I feel more in control. I can choose the career I want. I didn't even like my last job so it's not worth getting upset about. This could very well turn out for the best.*

Here's another scenario, where someone has simply misplaced their house keys.

Situation: *I can't find my keys and so I can't leave the house.*

Depressive train of thought: *I'm going to be late. I've let everyone down again. My brain is clearly failing. It's the depression doing this. I wouldn't be surprised if my brain has long-term damage from the constant mental fatigue.*

Mindset: *Exaggerating the predicament and assuming the worst.*

More positive train of thought: *We all forget things, especially when we are in a hurry and aren't paying enough attention. It's perfectly normal. Depression doesn't cause brain damage! It just affects my ability to think clearly. I'll retrace my steps from the time I came home and that should help me figure out where I last had them.*

Resulting mindset: *I'm going to research forgetfulness and brain deterioration with depression so I have all the facts. And I'm going to try to pay more attention to what I'm doing, to be present in the moment, when I feel stressed and distracted.*

Eliminate the negative

Being stuck in the depression blockage means being stuck with ongoing negative thoughts. But the goal is not to eliminate all negative thoughts. That would not be healthy. Negative thoughts can help us to realistically weigh the pros and cons of any situation. The trick is not to weight things too heavily in the negative. We need balance. What we do want to eliminate are any dominant negative thoughts that contribute to the depression blockage. We do this by consciously replacing it with a more positive thought. Let's look at a few examples.

Negative: *I'm overweight, diabetic, and I just can't seem to get control over my life. I've just lost another job and I'm going nowhere. I'm a total loser.*

Positive: There are plenty of more debilitating health issues than diabetes. This is a treatable health issue and I can see it as a motivator for getting healthy. It's my choice: either I stay the way I am and be miserable or take positive steps to feel better. I want to feel better.

Negative: *I am a failure. I can't hold down a job, I'm alone, and I'm unhappy all of the time.*

Positive: Success and failure are subjective. My definition of success doesn't have to match anyone else's. If I don't like myself, then I can change what I don't like. If I can be the kind of person I'd be proud to be, then I will probably attract more good people into my life. Instead of expecting life to hand me things, I need to focus on earning them for myself. I have nothing to lose! I'm going to start by volunteering at the local soup kitchen once a week.

Negative: *I should have done things differently. I'm always making the wrong decisions. I never do anything right.*

Positive: OK, I made a mistake, but the decision I made seemed valid at the time. I made the best decision I could with the information I had available to me. And there's no way of knowing how things would have turned out if I'd done something else. Instead, I can look at what I've learned from the experience so I can be smarter next time. I need to focus on a solution instead of beating myself up for the problem. Everyone has problems, not just me.

Goal setting

Goal setting is a powerful tool when you are caught in the depression blockage. By starting with broad goals and then narrowing these down to specific goals, you can rank and monitor them to track your progress. This will automatically give you more confidence.

Start first by setting broad goals and then refine each to a more specific goal to help you to develop more confidence in your progress. Remember, it is not so much about the destination as the journey. We are striving for slow and steady improvement, regardless of how long it takes to achieve the primary goal. If you focus solely on whether you achieve the primary goal, you can set yourself up for disappointment. With a depression blockage, you do not want to open the door to hopelessness stepping back inside. Here are some examples to get you started.

Broad goal	Broad timeframe	Specific goal	Satisfaction level (0–10)	Results
Become more positive	4 weeks	Start walking 30 minutes every morning; focus on my breathing and appreciating the beauty around me	7	This elevates my mood. I feel better doing it with a full stomach as I'm less tired afterwards.
Improve my fitness levels	3 months	Walk around the block every day until I can do it 3 times in 30 mins. Get a gym membership and train four times a week. Consider working with a personal trainer.	6	I managed 3 laps of a square block in 30 minutes after 2 weeks of consistent walking. I worked with a trainer for a couple of weeks to ensure I was working out safely and now I'm going to the gym 4 nights a week and can feel the difference. I'm stronger, I don't get out of breath easily anymore, and I find myself wanting to eat healthier foods because I feel so much better.

Broad goal	Broad timeframe	Specific goal	Satisfaction level (0–10)	Results
Be more social, less solitary	Call a different friend every day each week. Go out to eat either alone or with someone once a week.	To feel a lot more confident and at ease with doing this before the end of the month.	9	It was difficult at first but now it's getting easier to pick up the phone and call people. I've changed going out to eat to going to a coffee shop for budget and weight reasons and I turn off my mobile phone when we sit down so I can concentrate on our conversation. Sometimes making small talk is a challenge for me but I'm getting better at it now that I'm more relaxed and less self-conscious.

It is a good idea to keep a list of your progress because you will likely be amazed at how far you come in a relatively short period of time. It is easy to remember our failures vividly and forget or overlook our successes. Reward yourself for your achievements, such as buying yourself something new to wear once you start to slim down. Rewarding yourself helps to keep your outlook positive.

Recurrence

Being caught in the depression blockage can be devastating. And whilst getting out and uncovering stuckburies and unblocking is satisfying, it is important to be aware that you may experience them again. As noted in earlier chapters, changing habits is hard and takes time, and sometimes it can be a two steps forward, one step back kind of experience. If that happens, it helps to be prepared, to have an action plan when you find yourself getting stuck again. Believe me, I know. Years ago, I was stuck in the depression blockage. I lost my partner, my business, and life felt like a dark hole. I recovered using many of these techniques I'm sharing with you. I always had a Plan B in case I got caught in the black hole again. Here is the list of techniques I use.

1. **Immersion**
   Intuition is accomplished by being immersed in something. When I find something I love, I immerse myself in it. That takes the focus off the blockage and I begin to see the light again. The more passionate I am about something, the less insurmountable the blockage becomes.

2. **Flexibility**
   Things go wrong. I have to expect that. Part of that expectation is being flexible. Most days, I can bend and adjust.

3. **Appreciation/Gratitude**
   This is my most effective tool against slipping back into my depression blockage and can be done at any moment. There are always positive things I am grateful for.

4. **Communication ability**
   This is paramount. The better I am at expressing my thoughts, the better I am at getting good feedback. The feedback of communication falls into the basket of pinpointing accurate information and solutions.

5. **Importance**
   A friend of mine advised me, 'Always remember you are amazing, no matter how bad you think you are. You are on this planet for a reason and we have the ability to be as awesome as we want. We just have to believe that.'

6. **Purpose**
   Having a purpose is the reason why we go to bed and wake up each day. I identify my purpose and remind myself of it when I feel lost.

7. **Understanding**
   Now that I have traced my depression back to one (or more) painful incidents in my childhood, incidents that were not my fault, I can learn to manage those negative emotions effectively in stressful situations.

8. **Medication**
   If natural self-help remedies do not work and therapy is not enough, I can consult a mental health practitioner to see whether I might benefit from medication, which is often taken in conjunction with other therapies.

SUMMARY

- People with depressive block passively accept that something is wrong with them and the way their brain functions, and are convinced they will never fulfil their potential dreams and aspirations, instead of searching for lifestyle changes that could improve their situation.

- Depression can be associated with low moods that persist for a long time. When we have a low mood, we have a series of biased thinking methods that reinforce the depression blockage.

- Brisk walking helps to elevate moods, as it forces you to pay attention to what is outside of you.

- Setting realistic goals and tracking them helps you document your positive progress and serves as a great reminder as to how far you have come.

Blockage 5: The Negativity Blockage

> *The more you praise and celebrate your life, the more there is in life to celebrate.*
>
> — Oprah Winfrey

Ever wonder why some people seem to have a perpetually negative outlook? Newspapers and television news programmes are the same – you rarely hear about anything positive occurring. If the information that we gather is always negative, our world will fill with negative perceptions. Life is a battle between positive and negative energy. We must have both to exist, but life is about balance. With more negative than positive, an imbalance inevitably occurs.

Live longer – be less negative

Are you an optimist or a pessimist? Studies have shown that, on average, optimists live longer. Optimists are positive-minded people who look at life in ways that are rational and fulfilling. They are less deterred when negative situations arise. Pessimists, on the other hand, see life through a negative lens. They play the blame game, whether it is blaming themselves or others. Mistakes are magnified as disasters.

We are taught from an early age to be cautious, that attempting anything new or risky can be problematic or fail. The emphasis is on careful planning, to ensure nothing goes wrong. If it goes wrong, we are often reprimanded for failing, for not having a perfect plan in the first place.

From early childhood, our tendency is to consider the negative rather than the positive. According to Erik Erikson's theory of psychosocial development, 3–5 years of age is when children begin to make up games and initiate activities with other children. If allowed to do this, children develop a sense of initiative. They feel confident in their ability to make decisions and take the lead. If children are criticised or controlled, however, they become reluctant to try new things. Their creativity is stunted and they tend to become followers, rather than leaders.

Children between the ages of 5 and 12 years become more independent. They get involved in activities and doing things on their own. When encouraged in this, children develop confidence to succeed and believe that they are competent. If parents or teachers restrict activities and do not encourage children, they tend to feel inferior and doubt their own abilities.[14] These feelings of insecurity can be quite painful and often lead to a negativity blockage.

Parenting and negativity

Parents, particularly inexperienced parents, traditionally adopt the role of safeguarding their children, avoiding risk in order to keep their children safe, so even the most well-meaning parents can affect a child's confidence. Parents tell their children that they cannot, they should not, and they will not. Such children may not develop sufficient confidence in their own imaginations and often fail to develop their strengths and abilities. They are plagued by doubt about their ability to succeed. As a result, they fail to readily engage with life's challenges.

Living example of a negativity blockage

Anna is six. She is a happy child, courteous and confident. Anna's parents encourage her to try new things rather than focus on what she cannot do. Anna loves to help her mother in the kitchen and has learned to bake a cake almost entirely on her own, with minimal supervision. And although it is her least favourite part, she has been taught how to clean up after she is finished.

As a result, Anna is a confident little girl. She has learnt that she has the ability to accomplish things, and that trying new things is exciting and that mistakes are not disasters and so she learns from them. Anna is likely to become an adult who is confident in her ideas and her ability to make them a reality.

The negativity blockage focuses on what can go wrong at the expense of the positive. It is based on the fear of being wrong, and the negative consequences that can result, including being seen as inferior. Negativity-blocked people desperately need to ensure that nothing can go wrong, which can paralyse them into doing nothing.

The evolution of negative feelings

Evolutionary psychologist Roy Baumeister says that we are programmed to pay more attention to negative information than positive information, that we are attuned to danger, because our survival depends on it. And Dr Rick Hanson, a neuropsychologist, argues that our brains evolved in such a way that we are tricked into overestimating threats, underestimating opportunities, and underestimating resources.

Take, for example, a man who is anxious to secure a promotion. Initially, he might fear that a colleague is better suited to the position and will be offered the job instead – mistake number one, overestimating threats. Then he might downplay the job, preparing himself for his potential failure to secure the position – mistake number two, underestimating opportunities. Lastly, he convinces himself that he is not capable of doing the job well anyway – mistake number three, underestimating resources. Not only do we tend to exaggerate the negative but we underrate the positive opportunities available to us and our capability to succeed.

Indeed, when individuals are shown images that arouse neutral, positive, or negative feelings, they react most strongly to the images that evoke a negative response. We are hard-wired to notice more what we perceive to be negative than positive.

Moving forward

People with the negativity block are reluctant to move forward, preferring the safety of the tried and true. When they believe something is potentially negative, they see it as wholly negative – there is no upside. This difficulty in believing positives exist in a negative situation is a form of *cognitive dissonance*, the inability to consider opposing or conflicting thoughts at the same time.

Consider smokers who are addicted to smoking, whilst being fully aware of the habit's negative health implications. They find many reasons to justify their smoking, dismissing how it is unhealthy because that conflicts with their desire to smoke. They ignore what otherwise might make them entertain giving up smoking. Instead, they focus only on those reasons why they should continue smoking.

A person who tends to be negative reinforces his or her position by considering only those facts or perceptions that bolster that position, thereby becoming more negative. They cannot entertain any opposing thoughts, as they do not fit with their primary thought. Accordingly, if that negative mindset prevents someone from doing something, they will focus on even more negative thoughts later to support why they did not do it.

For example, if you are afraid to learn how to drive a car because you are unsure you are capable of coordinating all the controls whilst watching both the road and vehicles ahead and behind you, you will bolster that belief with other negative thoughts, such as falling victim to distracted or drunk drivers or unavoidably hitting an animal that bolts in front of you. With a negativity blockage, at no point do you balance that argument with the freedom and convenience that driving provides, or that your knowing how to drive could save a life rather than risk one. The negativity blockage blocks you from seeing anything but the negative in a situation.

Living example of a negativity blockage

Five years ago, Denzel broke up with his wife. He has two young daughters whom he sees every fortnight. He has a job that he stays in merely for the financial security. He is unhappy with it and complains constantly about his boss and co-workers, but he is convinced that he must stay in order to keep his pension.

Denzel often meets up with his friend Brian, who is now in the process of starting his own business, something he has often encouraged Denzel to do but Denzel refuses to even discuss it. Denzel starts talking about how bad the economy is and how it is probably not a good time to start a new business. Anything Brian shares, Denzel responds with a caution. Denzel is convinced he's helping his friend, but Brian is beginning to feel frustrated with him.

Brian changes the subject to how he and his partner are trying for a baby. Denzel shakes his head and reminds Brian that, speaking from experience, divorce rates have never been higher and how having children puts a great strain on a relationship, and asking how Brian thinks he is going to manage running a new business with parenting a newborn. 'You're setting yourself up for failure,' he warns Brian.

Consider the consequences of your negative thinking. The short-term and long-term consequences include physical, psychological, professional, and emotional. This will help to motivate you to do something about your negative thinking.

There are ways to redress the balance when thinking negatively, rather than positively. Focus on matching each negative with a positive. For instance, replace 'I don't want to go to the dentist because he is going to give me a needle and I hate needles' with 'If he doesn't give me a needle then it will hurt; the injection is designed to help me, to reduce my pain'. This affirms that wherever there is anything negative, there is always a positive – the cloud with the silver lining, if you will. By introducing and reinforcing positive thoughts, your view becomes more balanced, enabling you to move forward, attempting new things which may pleasantly surprise and encourage you when they succeed.

When you have a negative blockage, willing yourself to try something new that makes you nervous is by no means a small undertaking. But being prepared for eventualities and 'speed bumps' will help. It is called risk management. Having a backup strategy minimises the fears of what to do if and when something goes wrong. It is not a disaster; it is not the end of the world – you can deal with it. If you have a backup strategy, you will feel more comfortable taking action than if you are completely unprepared.

For example, if you fear bumping into an ex-partner at a social event, take some time to consider what options you have to manage the situation. You might bring a friend so that you are not caught on your own; you can practise what to say if suddenly faced with that person, as well as smiling and acting relaxed. The point is that you have options, and often the prospect of encountering something negative is far worse than the reality.

It is important to critically examine your negative thoughts. Ask yourself whether they are valid concerns or potentially overstated, even unrealistic. Having negative thoughts is not necessarily a bad thing, remember, as it does alert us to potential hazards. However, harbouring negative thoughts to the point where you are unable to advance or try new things hurts you.

Cognitive therapy

Cognitive therapy focuses on how our thoughts influence our moods, and recognising and correcting negative automatic thoughts. Over time, it can uncover and correct deeply held, false beliefs that contribute to your negativity block.

When you become consumed by thoughts of things that can go wrong, it prevents you from enjoying the present, and from taking part in things because you are convinced they will not work out. To address this negative thinking, focus on the present. Pay attention to the way your body feels. Use your senses to take in your surroundings. This interrupts your thoughts, disrupting the negative thinking pattern. When you notice that you are thinking negatively, meditation and mindfulness are both methods you can use.

The 3-1 principle

According to psychologist and bestselling author Barbara Fredrickson, we need to string together three positive emotions in order to fight off one negative emotion. This is because, as mentioned earlier, the brain is wired to assign more importance to a negative thought or perception than a positive one.[15]

It takes more than just deciding to be positive to make it happen. Being open, curious, appreciative, kind, genuine, and sincere generates positive emotions. When we are open and real to our circumstances, great things are easier to see.

Being real is particularly important. In her 2011 article, 'Are You Getting Enough Positivity in Your Diet?', Fredrickson advises not to 'pump too much sunshine into our lives'. What she means is to avoid taking it to the extreme. For example, if you were to reply 'Fantastic!' every single time someone asks, 'How's it going?' how often would that response be realistic? No one has a fantastic day every day. We all go through rough spots and get over tough times. They cannot be avoided altogether. The goal is to monitor your emotions so that you can inject more positivity when you realise that your feelings are trending steadily negative.

Applying the 3–1 Principle can help you to become more positive. How? The next time you get stuck in the negativity blockage, go and do three things that generate three positive emotions in you – joy, happiness, contentment, satisfaction: take a brisk walk through the park, listen to your favourite music, go shopping, engage in random acts of kindness. Keep a log of what things you try, how they made you feel, and how effective they were at changing you from a negative outlook to a positive one.

Follow your passion

It is difficult to be negative when you are passionate about something. It gives your life purpose, which in itself is positive. The more positive emotions we have, the less likely we are to be chronically pessimistic. When we are passionate and believe in a cause, time is used wisely, which includes mind power time. When we are busy doing something we believe in, we do not have time to think of anything negative.

Inspiration precludes being negative. Research shows that when reading inspiring stories, brain activity changes and chemicals are released. In times of despair, recalling an inspirational story can boost positive emotions.

Words influence your thoughts

When we spend our time primarily being negative, we express ourselves in negative generalisations. We make blanket statements like 'Life is always a struggle', 'The world is a dangerous place', or 'Everyone is dishonest'. Uttering those statements repeatedly reinforces a negative outlook. Try to catch yourself when you make statements like that. Be specific instead of making sweeping statements. Even shifting 'Everyone is dishonest' to 'Some people are just dishonest' sends a subtle message to your brain that if some people are dishonest, then there are still plenty of people who are honest. It is a more positive approach. The more you can narrow your scope when making a negative observation, the less negative it will feel.

Envy and greed

Feelings of envy and greed, or covetousness, are examples of extremely negative thinking that will continue to hold you back until you can break the pattern. Have you ever resented the fact that someone you know drives a nicer car than you do? Or felt angry because everyone around you seems to be in a successful relationship whilst you go home every night feeling miserable and lonely?

The best way to break these thought patterns is to use the appreciation/gratitude approach. When you find yourself having an uncharitable or resentful thought about someone, stop yourself, take a breath, and then think of why you are grateful for what you have.

Negative: *John has such a huge, impressive home whilst I live in this dinky one-bedroom apartment.*

Positive: *John has such a huge, impressive home. I'd love to live in a house like that someday, but right now I'm actually better off in my apartment because I want to save money and it gives me more free time to pursue activities I enjoy. If I had a home like that, my expenses would be a lot higher and I'd be spending all my time working to pay for it. Nope, I'm much happier where I am right now!*

Adopting a positive perspective like the one above involves countering a negative perspective with a positive. It takes time, practice, and persistence to change these habits, but the things worth doing most are the things that require effort, the things that do not come easily. Try not to get discouraged. With practice, it gets easier and easier, to where you will find yourself interrupting a negative thought mid-sentence and reorienting yourself without having to struggle to find something positive to say.

Certain words and phrases can set you up to be more negative than positive. The word 'should' and phrases like 'if only' are stress-inducing. *I should call my friend today* implies a reluctance and sense of obligation whereas *I'm going to call my friend this evening* gives you a specific goal and changes a feeling of obligation to one of anticipation.

See if you can identify what words and phrases you tend to use that put you in a negative frame of mind. Jot them down and set yourself a goal, starting with doing it over the course of a single day, to avoid using those phrases. If you catch yourself doing it, don't berate yourself. Remember, these are habits, and habits are hard to break. Simply smile and try to reword what you were thinking or saying into a more positive framework.

Boiling anger

Do you tend to let things fester inside you until it is impossible to hold it in any longer and you explode? Whilst anger is a normal emotion that we all experience, letting anger build up inside you, turning you into a volcano ready to blow, instead of finding a way to express it constructively, can only hurt you, as well as those around you.

A mentor of mine likens anger to energy that builds up inside you the same way steam builds up in a boiling pot. You are less likely to get burned, or burn anyone else, if you carefully let the steam escape a little at a time or turn off the fire beneath the pot and let it cool off before you open it.

It is possible to resolve building anger through meditation, breathing, or exercise. These allow you to focus your thinking away from what is angering you and towards the activity until your negativity subsides. By switching the fire off, you can switch your train of thought to something more positive.

Smile and empathise. It is difficult to be negative when you are smiling and being empathetic. For the next few weeks, smile every time you have a negative thought. See if it makes a difference. Try empathising with people who annoy you and see how you feel.

Living example of a negativity blockage

Mike and Jerry have been mates for a long time. Mike constantly tells Jerry what to do and what not to do. Jerry bites back about advice on girls or business. It causes arguments between them and then they stop talking to each other. When they catch up again, things are good at first, but inevitably they start to argue.

Jerry gets fed up with Mike. But this time he decides to smile every time Mike gives him advice. He feels empathy for him. He knows that other things are making Mike angry.

Astonishingly, the conversations start to change. Mike no longer seems so judgemental of Jerry. They start enjoying each other's company. Mike finds it difficult to be as negative and judgemental when Jerry practises empathy and smiles more. It brings out the best in Mike.

Unrealistic expectations

No one is perfect, including you. By giving yourself and others some slack, it becomes easier to see the positive side in situations and avoid unnecessary feelings of guilt. We are all human and mistakes occur. They are part of everyday life. Accepting yourself and others for who you and they are can be helpful in reducing negativity.

Guilt can be constructive as it can urge us to right a wrong we have done. However, guilt can create a downward spiral if you refuse to forgive yourself for a mistake you've made. Guilt can also be used as a form of punishment, when you refuse to forgive someone else's behaviour. Forgiveness and acceptance of others is about finding peace within yourself by not harbouring anger or resentment towards someone else.

Forgiving someone is not the same as condoning their negative or hurtful behaviour. You can forgive without forgetting. Forgiving is about letting go of the negative response inside you; it is not about pretending the hurtful action never occurred. Often the most difficult form of forgiveness is forgiving ourselves, and yet if we can forgive and accept ourselves, weaknesses and all, we find it easier to forgive and accept others. And that brings real peace.

Choose your companions wisely

Likes attract. If you are primarily negative, you will attract and be attracted to others who support your way of thinking. Breaking the habit of negativity means surrounding yourself with positive-minded people. They are an excellent constant reminder of your goal to be more positive and can be constructive role models.

SUMMARY

- When children are criticised or controlled, they become fearful in showing initiative.

- We react more strongly to information we perceive as negative than that which we view as positive.

- When a person is paralysed into avoiding taking action in life out of fear of what could go wrong, and instead insist on playing it safe, they are suffering a negativity blockage.

- People with a negativity blockage doubt their abilities and are afraid to take risks that might improve their lives. Being passionate and creative can help reverse this belief system.

- Guilt, anger, envy, greed, and resentment, if left to build up inside, magnifies and reinforces negativity, as does surrounding yourself with negative-minded people.

- It is difficult to harbour negative thoughts when your thoughts are focused on the positive, and vice versa. When you focus on the positive, you can shift your thought patterns.

Blockage 6: The Victim Blockage

> *As you grow older, you will discover that you have two hands, one for helping yourself, the other for helping others.*
>
> — Audrey Hepburn

Do you find yourself regularly feeling frustrated with your life? Do you feel helpless to make things better or blame others or circumstances for what is holding you back?

If so, you may be suffering a victim blockage, where you feel like you are a victim to circumstances and are helpless to change your situation. It is the hardest blockage to treat and beat, and is the one that has given me the most trouble in my life.

It can resemble the negativity blockage but the negativity in this instance always surrounds the person being put upon and how, selectively, their life is bad but not anyone else's. It is a passive outlook. Life becomes an unending litany of tales of woe, excuses, and rationalisations. Whilst masters of their destiny go out and make things happen, victims sit and wait.

Whether you are a victim or a master depends upon your *locus of control*, the extent to which you believe you have control over the events that affect you. If you take responsibility for what happens to you and believe that hard work combined with your own abilities is what generates positive outcomes, then you have an internal locus of control.

In contrast, if you tend to blame people and things outside of yourself for your problems and do not feel you shoulder any of the responsibility for what happens to you, you have an external locus of control.[16] People with the victim blockage do not think to change their behaviour in hopes of influencing an outcome, and in fact are reluctant to do so.

Children who grow up in a neglectful and harsh family environment can develop a victim blockage. When parents are overly critical or indifferent, children find they get more support and attention when they are miserable or suffering.

Abused children on the other hand learn to equate intimacy with harm. As adults, they look to recreate intimacy by replicating the unhealthy situations of their childhood. They only feel loved when they are mistreated. As children, they are powerless to stop the abuse. When they become adults, they continue to feel powerless, regardless of their situation, and often express their repressed anger towards their parents through self-sabotaging behaviour.[17]

Living example of a victim blockage

Sophie's parents separated when she was four years old. Whilst concerned about the effects this might have on Sophie, her parents were busy professionals and often distracted.

To gain attention, Sophie became a naughty child, and cried every time she was disciplined. Feeling guilty about the separation, her parents would immediately comfort her. Sophie quickly learnt that crying resulted in attention and affection from her parents far more effectively than good behaviour.

In school, Sophie found studying difficult and would cry in front of her teacher when she received a bad grade or was criticised in any way. After graduation, she moved from job to job because whenever difficulties arose, she would become distressed and give up.

> Sophie subconsciously self-sabotages to get attention instead of working through her difficulties. Sophie's romantic relationships are also volatile as she uses the same techniques to demand her partner's attention and affection.

Individuals with a victim blockage willingly relinquish control over their lives. They seek attention but do not wish to resolve their problems, as that would require active change on their part. Some suggestions can be met with outright hostility and accusations of harm. Their life becomes a cycle where things go from bad to worse. People stuck in the victim blockage see no way out and feel they have no options.

The victim mindset

A person with the victim blockage has a mindset that does not allow for much positive progress. Why is this? They see several benefits in their behaviour:

- Immediate expressions of sympathy – you receive comfort from people who are concerned and express willingness to help.

- Life is safe – you tend to take no action, which translates to no risk of failure or rejection.

- Life is passively easy – you take no responsibility for what happens in life, avoiding making difficult decisions or having to work hard towards your goals.

- You are always innocent – you are right and everyone else is wrong.

Studies show that people with a victim blockage, who possess an external locus of control, are likely to suffer from depression, feelings of powerlessness, helplessness, and hopelessness.[18] Why?

Because people are happiest when they recognise their ability to affect what happens in life whilst understanding that they cannot control everything.[19] People with a balanced mindset, accepting both what they can and cannot control, tend to be the happiest.[20] People who focus on what they can achieve, rather than what they cannot achieve, tend to be far more successful.

Living example of a victim blockage

Ludwig is 55. He was laid off 15 years ago and has been stuck in the victim blockage ever since.

His friends felt sorry for him when he was retrenched. When Ludwig missed out on a job opportunity, his friends consoled him. When Ludwig broke his leg, he could not attend job interviews so his friends helped him. When offered suggestions for improving his life, he would give reasons why such solutions to his problems would never work.

Ludwig began to self-sabotage by sleeping in, staying up late, and not bothering to look for work. No time was a good time to apply for work, as far as he was concerned.

He complains to get attention and self-sabotages to avoid the fears and doubts he feels when trying to accomplish something.

How to unblock yourself

How do you stop being a victim and take control of your life? You start by taking full responsibility for everything that happens to you. This can be difficult, but it is by no means impossible. If a person can accept responsibility for their actions, they establish a greater sense of control over what happens to them. They can better perceive their possible contribution to a given situation. It can help to consider why other people's behaviour affects them the way it does.

Ask yourself this: Who is responsible for the quality of your life? Is it your partner, your kids, society, your neighbour, your best friend, your boss, your history, your parents? If your answer does not include yourself as responsible in any way, you think like a victim.

Responsibility

We all take ownership for our wins in life. For example, if you get a promotion at work, you celebrate your hard work and how much you merit it. You deserve the win and you take full responsibility. We all take responsibility for success, but what about failure? It is a struggle to take responsibility for failure when you are stuck in the victim blockage.

Emotions need to be examined and responsibility taken. You are the one who generates those emotions, so you have to take responsibility, rather than expecting others to do so. We all need to take responsibility for our mishaps every day.

By taking responsibility, even for mishaps, you prepare for the unexpected. If you bought a car and it was faulty, then it is your responsibility to do whatever it takes to make things right.

You also need to take responsibility for your circumstances. For example, where you live, the job you have, your family, your financial position… These are all circumstances of life and they are no one else's responsibility above yours.

Relationships

The relationship is possibly the most overused scapegoat for victims. Victims love to point the finger. However, when you throw in the word 'choice', you start to make progress. If you cannot control something, then you still have choices. For example, if you cannot control an angry outburst, you still can *choose* to do the right thing afterwards. You can even choose the thoughts you want to use.

If, for example, as a teenager you have suffered abuse, you can passively hold onto the story of that abuse that keeps you right where you are in life. Or you can choose not to define yourself by the abuse you received and instead take responsibility for changing your life in a way that is more constructive.

We have choices. We can choose one road or another, different journeys with different destinations. Even the things you cannot control you can still control in terms of how you perceive them, and the ways in which you react to and deal with them. You can control your feelings by knowing which thoughts and feelings you choose to experience.

People who get caught in the victim blockage often feel overwhelmed and tired because they expend lots of energy in telling people how bad things are. Their brain and cell make-up gets fatigued. If you keep saying how difficult something is, your whole body will adhere to the energy drop and feel exhausted.

Your body is remarkably engaged in your thoughts. If it is positively linked, it can wake you up, and lift you from fatigue into energy. Imagine living your day with negative charges. Your whole body will be negatively charged every day. After some time, this takes its toll on all your organs and your body in general.

Victims are also the kings of excuses. The excuses need to stop and the giving needs to start. When victims start giving, excuses end. They feel empowered at the prospect of giving again.

It is important to take responsibility for how you react and what you do – or do not do – to overcome an obstacle. Anything that happens to you is your responsibility to address.

Blaming and carrying on does not fix things; it only makes a situation worse. If serious things have happened, you need to deal with them and move on. If they are your stuckburies, explore what caused them to develop. Identify how your blockages formed and when they started to impact your life. Instead of blaming the past, you will be addressing it. By addressing it, you start to make some progress.

We have control over the way we perceive and react to something. This is where the victim gains consciousness of life's experiences and comes out of his or her shell. It is about personal growth.

One of the most important things a person with the victim blockage mindset can do is to stop complaining. When a person complains, they reinforce their sense of helplessness and hopelessness.

Instead, a person with this mindset can focus their attention on what can be done to improve the situation. If they are upset about it, how can they prevent it from happening again? It can also help to reflect upon what they have to feel grateful for. This may help to shift perspective on a situation.

By recognising positive aspects of life, a person can get a sense of what they have, not what they don't. A person with this mindset can think about whether there is a hidden opportunity. This can help focus upon what needs to be done to experience a benefit. Also, the question of how a person can add value in a situation helps a person discover their control. Answering this question directs behaviour towards a goal.

The ego is part of the conscious and unconscious mind. It experiences the outside world and reacts to it. The ego resists change. This reaction to change is based on the unconscious fear that a person is not good enough to succeed at anything. It prevents a person from accepting new information that challenges the status quo. To help counteract the ego's resistance to change, a person can expose themselves to both new and different ideas and beliefs.

As we learned earlier in this chapter, a person with an internal locus of control believes that what happens in life is a result of their own efforts. By recognising that behaviours contribute to circumstances, a person feels more control over their environment. A person can start by setting small goals to work towards and achieve. Self-confidence in a person's ability to influence their circumstances will improve as goals are achieved.

A person can take action to change a situation they are unhappy with. For example, if living in a messy house, taking steps to clean the house. After a change in behaviour, a person may notice that the situation, too, has changed for the better.

Cognitive behavioural therapy, which involves talking with a medical professional to challenge negative thoughts so that changes in behaviour are brought about, can assist in improving the victim blockage mindset, as it combats unhelpful thoughts and perceptions about stressful events. It can help someone with this mindset to understand how their behaviour, or changes to their behaviour, can lead to positive results.

Destructive thoughts make a person feel helpless and discourage them from taking action to change a situation. It is helpful to identify these thoughts. If a person with the victim blockage mindset can challenge destructive thoughts, they may feel less distressed and also more powerful in situations. Also, a person with this mindset will likely feel more empowered by using *I can* and *I will* statements. Such statements motivate a person to initiate behaviour.

Another important way to address this mindset is to turn the focus outward and consider what can be done to help somebody else. The way a person treats others has a big effect on the way they treat themselves.

Step outside your comfort zone

By doing things differently, you automatically empower yourself. It is hard to do this when you see yourself as a victim. In doing things differently, you step outside of your comfort zone and break away from being a victim. You do not need that big new happening to occur; you will see and feel it in the small changes. Those will be the stepping stones to continue onward.

Reading some great books or watching a great movie can be just the thing to motivate you to move forward.

Identify something that typically upsets you and decide to react differently. For example, when people cancel on you and your immediate reaction is that this always happens to you, and you alone, turn it around and take responsibility for how you react. Call someone else to join you instead.

Apologise sincerely

Saying 'I'm sorry I screamed at you, but I've had a bad day' is not the same thing as taking responsibility for your behaviour. Saying 'I'm sorry I screamed at you' takes responsibility. The 'but' kills the apology. Do not try to assess blame elsewhere. Shoulder it.

Focus on others instead of yourself

By helping people, you shift attention away from you and onto someone else. You cannot be a victim when you help someone; instead, you become the master of your life. The more you love other people, the more you love yourself.

SUMMARY

- When parents are overly critical or indifferent, children learn that symptoms of acute distress can often evoke sympathy and gain them the desired attention.

- People who get caught in the victim blockage expend too much of their energy by complaining.

- People with the victim blockage believe they have no control over what happens in their lives. This belief prevents them from taking action and making changes to their behaviour.

- People with the victim blockage ask for help only because they seek pity and want attention.

- People with the victim blockage do not believe that changing their behaviour influences outcomes. They ignore genuine help, or undermine it when it is offered.

- The first step to improving the victim blockage mindset is to take responsibility for how you react to what happens in your life.

- Cognitive behavioural therapy can help a person to question thoughts about stressful events. It can help a person to understand how control impacts their life in positive ways.

Blockage 7: The 'Shiny Ball' Blockage

> *Whatever it takes to finish things, finish. You will learn more from a glorious failure than you ever will from something you never finished.*
>
> — Neil Gaiman

Do you know someone who starts something but never finishes it? They are enthusiastic in the beginning, but when the excitement tapers off, they move on to something else?

Picture a young child sitting in a room full of brand new colourful balls. The child picks one and goes outside to play with it. When the ball becomes dirty, the child discards it, goes back inside, and picks another ball to play with. When that ball gets dirty, the child tosses it aside and goes back to get a clean one. It continues like this until there are no more shiny balls left, at which point they lose interest.

Does this sound like you? You start a new project and it is exciting, emotionally stimulating, and extremely motivating. Maybe you even become a bit obsessed by it. At first, the new venture seems perfect and full of promise. You pay no attention to the possible obstacles or challenges. After a while, this new activity requires more effort than first thought, the novelty wears off, and, bored, you turn your attention to something new.

Starting something new is not unlike falling in love, according to Dr Susan Perry in her Psychology Today blog post '5 Ways to Finish What You Start (and Why You Often Don't)'[21]. Initially, when you fall for someone, they are perfect in your eyes, totally engaging, and you want to spend every minute you have with them. Over time, when reality intrudes, you start to become aware of the person's habits and idiosyncrasies.

Now, in a healthy relationship, that does not present a problem, but to someone with a shiny ball blockage, they are perhaps more in love with the infatuation, the magic, than with the actual person. So, when the magic fades and the day-to-day realities of living become more evident, and the relationship begins to require some effort, if you have this blockage you might find your attention wandering, hoping to discover someone else who can spark that same effortless magic.

Living example of a shiny ball blockage

Jarryd grew up an adventurous child and his parents willingly indulged his curiosities. When he abandoned anything, they would swoop in and clean up the mess. When he grew old enough to do chores, he quickly realised that if he left a chore half done, instead of scolding or punishing him, Jarryd's mother would simply finish the task without a word. He was free to move on to something more interesting. If a school project proved more difficult than first expected, his father would step in. 'Let me,' he'd say, and finish the job.

As a result, Jarryd never learned the art of persistence or the value of hard work. There was always one of his parents standing by, waiting to pick up where he left off.

This learnt behaviour prevents a person from completing anything. It also has ramifications for people they involve in their ventures. By moving to another project, the first project gets let down. Similarly, people in the new project will eventually be let down, because at some point, the new project will be dropped.

The shiny ball blockage is an attempt to avoid the difficult feelings that arise when trying to achieve something that requires more time and effort than anticipated, and causes someone to drop that in favour of something else when challenges arise because it seems easier and more attractive, be it a project, a person, or an opportunity.

The shiny ball blockage is a way of avoiding or distracting yourself from your own problems. At some point, when you try to succeed at anything, you are confronted by your own fears and doubts. Perhaps you are confronted by a fear that you are not capable of succeeding. Or perhaps you are scared that you do not deserve to succeed. These painful feelings can be dodged when you swiftly move on to something else instead.

The underlying purpose of the shiny ball blockage is to avoid dealing with your stuckburies when they surface. By distracting yourself with something new, you get short-term relief from the difficult feelings you experience when trying to succeed and instead become enthralled with the idea that an easier path to success is around the corner. The grass is always greener on the other side of the fence.

What defines people with the shiny ball blockage is how quickly they change direction and take on new projects whilst often achieving nothing. Yet, they scoff at others who do persist, insisting they are unimaginative, fearful of taking chances, and perhaps even cowardly.

Techniques to unblock

People with the shiny ball blockage benefit from setting themselves small, easy-to-achieve goals to start off with before setting slightly more challenging goals that take a little more time to achieve. This reinforces the satisfaction experienced from seeing a job through, from start to finish.

Choosing to work closely with people who finish what they start is one way to help do this. A person with the shiny ball blockage could team up with a detail-oriented person who is willing to help them. You may find that, in a business partnership, one partner is the creative one, always looking for new ideas, whilst the other partner is the pragmatic one, who analyses the ideas, decides which to pursue, and does all the necessary behind the scenes work to realise the creative partner's vision.

Unfortunately, most people with the shiny ball blockage do not want to do the work they need to do on themselves. They often fail to commit themselves to a reliable partner. Instead they just keep moving from project to project, never getting sufficient results to reward them for their effort and investment.

It helps for people with a shiny ball blockage to organise their activities and work out a plan for completing something. They can ensure that enough time and resources are allocated to finish each project. Having a plan like this offsets the natural tendency to spend a lot of time and money on something in the beginning.

By adhering to a plan, a person with the shiny ball blockage can avoid the tendency to lose interest in a project or abandon it because they have run out of resources due to lack of planning. It can assist them to manage their tasks and time effectively, as this is an area of weakness for them. By following their plan, they may be able to complete a project successfully.

Prioritising can be an important thing to do. However, it is essential to prioritise objectives. When a person achieves one of these objectives, it is a great source of motivation to go on and achieve the next objective.

People with shiny ball blockage need to focus on one thing at a time. They need to hold back on starting something new until they have completed their current project. They need to consider what is necessary to do something well and see it through to the end. By holding themselves to do this, they will learn how encouraging it is to succeed.

Attending counselling sessions for workaholics could help to prioritise their interests. The sessions will quickly get to the underlying cause for their behaviour, which is what the person is trying so hard to avoid.

When we examine patterns and lessons, we can work out the shiny ball blockage. People with shiny ball blockage rarely realise they act this way. When they do realise, they may become purposefully distracted, so that they do not pay attention to it. By listening to your feelings, emotions, and intuition, you generally see patterns. Being honest and present with yourself is pure magic when it comes to healing.

Self-image

Many times, the shiny ball syndrome can be attributed to the ability or potential to change your mood and improve self-image. Whilst shopping can and does improve self-image and self-evaluation, the effect wears off. Those who are obsessive, always searching for that next purchase, are addicted and in need of the next buzz.

Scientifically, focusing on your body's ability, and not its image, has been found to help a person's confidence. Research has shown that having cosmetic surgery does not make you feel significantly more confident or attractive afterwards. Focusing on what you have accomplished in life gives you the ability to stabilise and be happy with who you are.

External triggers

The best remedy and behaviour for shiny ball blockage healing is to focus internally. One tactic is be on the lookout for negatively manipulative people. For example, if you have someone who bases their self-worth on image, you may be manipulated into thinking like them. If you are caught in the shiny ball blockage, you may take buying to a new level and just keep buying to get the stimulus you require.

Avoid signs and advertisements designed to lure you in. Seeing a young man in a sports car may entice an older man to want to retain his youth by buying that car. This may equate to looking young again, and possibly attracting younger women.

If you are addicted to shopping, a great way to distinguish between true needs and simple wants is to write them down. If your wants far outweigh your needs, then you know you have a serious problem. Your wants should always represent a fraction of your needs.

Patience

People in the shiny ball blockage are impatient, but they do not know it. They need to address practising patience. Patience is about managing emotions and forcing yourself to slow down. It is a matter of being distracted from the thought that is manifesting within. You may disengage from the thought by breathing, meditating, or talking to other people. You need to get a solid distraction. Removing the tension you are holding will enable you to freely deal with the emotion, and the required patience should be more achievable.

Meditation and mindfulness

Meditation and staying in the present moment (instead of letting your attention wander to what other shiny objects might be within reach) is powerful therapy for anyone with the shiny ball blockage. You can move from a position of wants and needs to kindness and giving. This will help eliminate the materialism and allow you to count your blessings.

Focusing on spiritual concerns makes you more aware of what you already have and allows you to be grateful for it all. You think about the things that have helped you to be more fulfilled. Similar to meditation, include prayer – being thankful for the things you have experienced. Move into a position of sharing and giving acts of kindness.

Kindness is a gift that we have been given to give to others. We can use kindness to bring more pleasure to our lives and the lives of others. When you are kind and helpful to others, it brings joy and combines with spirituality. Spirituality, and giving kindness to others, gives you that special type of connection and appreciation for the world and people around you.

By simply breathing and connecting with the present and noticing your breathing, you can tap into your inner happiness storage. You start to feel your heartbeat, nature, the air, etc. When you connect, you start to develop your spirituality. It is a distraction from the hustle and bustle of getting a new buzz from starting new projects or buying things. Your buzz now comes from within.

You need to work to a place where you have no fear, where you enjoy the connection. Separation is an unhappy place, whilst connection is a happy place. You no longer have to publicise an image.

Deepak Chopra, in his book *The Seven Spiritual Laws of Success*, talks about the law of giving and receiving. If you want something, then you give something. I live by this law. If you want love, then you must give love. The intention behind your giving is what is important.

When we are joyful about the act of giving, and it is unconditional and from the heart, then the energy is positive and rewarding. When you give in a doubting or grudging way, then energy does not work in your favour.

Goal setting

Goals are important. (Part 3 discusses the principle of 'crystal clear purpose' in more depth.) Goals are determined by your purpose. The most important thing to remember is that goals keep you on track to your purpose in life. When you have goals, it may be less tempting to give into the shiny ball blockage, because you are adhering to your purpose. Your goals will force you to stay on track, but, of course, it is a matter of sticking to the goals and the purpose.

When you begin new projects, you feel energetic and enthusiastic. That energy slowly fades when you get into the intricacy of things. Look at the purpose and the result. This vision will give you the necessary drive and longevity. When you start and stop, you will find that the energy is all in the beginning because you are energetic with excitement. Just keep the end result in mind.

Tracking your progress

When you track your results and progress, this keeps you on track with your goals. It inhibits you from starting too many projects and getting off track. You will know when it happens.

In addition to tracking yourself daily, perhaps with a to-do list, it is important to review your progress on a larger scale, starting with weekly reviews. Look at the basics of your final goal and achievement versus target. This is particularly important in business, especially a new business. I have a sales system that shows me how much potential business is being gathered. Even though I may not get a sale, I am still motivated by what may come in the future. You can see the results without getting the sales results.

Doing this gives you something to focus on that shows your optimistic potential and makes you accountable to yourself. Accountability gives you responsibility and control. Additionally, this gives you a new sense of power that rivals repeatedly buying new and expensive objects.

You are your own shiny object. You do not need to find a new shiny object – you shine daily. All you need to do is to review and shine away.

SUMMARY

- The shiny ball blockage is essentially a short-term attention span, where a person moves from one venture to the next without completing anything. It is a way of distracting yourself from, or avoiding, unresolved emotional issues.

- A person with the shiny ball blockage has no need for more and more of what they already have. They need to stick with something long enough to accomplish and appreciate it.

- Shiny ball blockage people are likely to judge and ridicule others who are different to them, which is motivated by fear.

- By adhering to a plan, a person with the shiny ball blockage can avoid the tendency to abandon a project, or be left without sufficient resources to finish it.

- Partnering with practical and detail-oriented people may help a person with the shiny ball blockage to finish what they start.

Blockage 8: The Stress Blockage

> *We cannot solve our problems with the same thinking we used when we created them.*
>
> Albert Einstein

Stress is not the villainous vampire it is traditionally made out to be. In fact, stress can be a valuable motivator, urging us to solve problems and move forward. However, too much stress is not a good thing, and studies reveal that stress levels in this millennium are reportedly double that of just fifty or sixty years ago, before today's technology and unrealistic expectations of multitasking became a way of life.[22]

Why do some people worry more than others? Worry and stress are closely related and can dramatically influence each other. Worry is a constant concern about a particular thing or person, whilst stress is the overwhelming feeling of being responsible for something or someone. As humans, our brains are always on the lookout for threats. This searching process is fear-based, as there is always an element of danger in anything we do.

Insecurities lie at the root of worry, whether it is fear of an inability to do something, hold onto someone or a job, a parent's fear of not being able to protect their child every minute of the day – generally it stems from fears of an inability to control one's environment.

Take starting a business. If you spend all your time worrying about the economy, clients, interest, rates, and whatever else is out of your control, you risk the business failing because your chronic negativity prevents you from doing what you need to do to sustain it successfully.

Research has shown that when people who are under considerable stress face making a difficult decision, they have a tendency to focus more on the advantages gained by those decisions than the disadvantages, most likely in an attempt to reduce their stress level. So, someone who is stressing over whether to accept a job offer might place more emphasis on the potential increase in salary versus the unrealistic job targets they would be required to meet.

When a child grows up in a high-stress environment where parents act inconsistently, making it difficult for the child to know what constitutes good behaviour, it is confusing. A stress blockage develops where the individual is unable to determine how to confidently react to and resolve stressful situations.

Your body's reaction to stress

The General Adaptation Syndrome model, which describes the body's response to stress, was adapted from Hans Selye's research findings. In the initial alarm stage, the body responds to a stressful situation by releasing stress hormones that allow the body to protect itself. This is the body's 'fight or flight' response system.[23]

In the second stage, called the resistance stage, the body weakens as energy is diverted to repair muscles after the 'fight or flight' response. The body stays alert in case it needs to continue fighting.[24]

The third stage is the exhaustion phase, when the body is exhausted, overloaded with stress and drained of energy. People with the stress blockage are stuck in this exhaustion phase, because they are continually stressed.[25]

Stressed parents approach their children in inconsistent ways, depending upon how they feel. For example, a child is praised one day and the following day is punished for the same behaviour. The child guesses whether their behaviour is right or wrong. They cannot work this out from their parent's behaviour. These children take responsibility for their parent's unpredictable reactions, even though it has nothing to do with them. The child feels responsible for something they have no control over.[26]

As adults, these people get stressed about both what they can and cannot control. Their life is basically in turmoil, constantly consumed by stress. The person is reliving stressful situations from the past, where they felt an excess of responsibility without sufficient control. Their coping mechanism when encountering stressful situations is to shoulder more responsibility than they should, whilst feeling they can do little about the situation.

Living example of a stress blockage

Trudi worked in a publishing house and was recently promoted to a new job, a job where expectations of her turned out to be higher than she had anticipated or been led to believe. The work environment was fast-paced and stressful at the best of times. Trudi was drowning in work and could not achieve what was expected of her.

It did not occur to Trudi to sit down with her boss to address the situation. Instead, Trudi felt responsible, convinced the situation was her doing, but had no ability to change the situation on her own – the responsibility for change lay with her boss. But she was unable to see that, having spent her life feeling responsible for everything and everyone. She kept her head down and tried harder. It was not enough and Trudi was eventually fired. She left, feeling ashamed and responsible for what she assumed she had failed to do right.

The stress blockage is when stress completely confuses or distorts a person's focus and they are unable to achieve their goals or make good decisions. They become stuck in their ongoing experience of stress, becoming depleted of energy. People with the stress blockage cannot achieve their goals because they are disadvantaged for a number of reasons: research shows long-term stress causes concentration loss, people become inefficient and accident-prone, and memory is impaired.[27]

Chronic anxiety

Severe anxiety can have significant health implications, including leading to drug or alcohol dependence. There are constructive ways to defuse anxiety. One of them is practising mindfulness. Another comes under the realm of acceptance theory.

Acceptance theory is about accepting your thoughts as just that: your thoughts. And thoughts can change and be changed. They do not define you and are not always logical or grounded in reality.

For example, what if you left the heat up too high on the stove and burnt the dinner? You might think, 'I need to be more careful and pay attention to what I'm doing. I guess we'll be ordering pizza tonight'. But if you feel stressed, you might beat yourself up about it unnecessarily, thinking perhaps, 'What an idiot I am!' or 'I'm hopeless. I can't even get dinner right'.

The circumstances are the same – the difference lies in how you perceive those circumstances and whether you feel unnecessarily guilty or responsible for the part you played because you are a perfectionist, or whether you can laugh it off and say, 'Oh well, stuff happens!'

Let's say you go for a walk with a friend. You say something that you realise has offended him, based on his reaction, but he laughs it off and tells you not to worry. Yet, when you call him the next day, he does not answer. You immediately react as if you are responsible. You think back to what you said and you start to worry. Maybe he was not honest with you about how he reacted. Maybe now that he has had time to think about it, he is angry. You call again, twice, and still there is no answer. You call again the next day and he still does not reply. Now you are frantic, convinced that you have ended your friendship and you do not know what to do. So you jump into your car and drive over to his house to apologise, hoping he will forgive you. He opens the door, bleary-eyed, pale, and in his pyjamas. It turns out that he had woken up the day after he saw you with the flu and was too sick to answer the phone. You spent the past two days worrying yourself sick, convinced you were the reason he had not taken your call when in fact you had nothing to do with it.

When you are stress-sensitive, your mind quickly jumps to conclusions without evidence. But thoughts are just thoughts, and not always an accurate reflection of what's going on. We tend to forget this when a potential crisis occurs.

The way to resolve this is to increase the amount of time you spend in rest and recreation in order to reduce stress. It is important to find activities to spend your time that make you feel buoyant rather than worried, *and do them consistently*.

It is generally accepted that exercise reduces stress. We all have different exercise styles, so what kind of exercise is best? Research by Firdaus Dhabhar, of Stanford Medical School, suggests that regular brisk walks may be better than inconsistent high-energy exercise. If we adopt this sort of regime, it makes regular exercise easy for most of us.[28]

Incessant worry

In Blockage 4, I quoted one of Shakespeare's famous lines from *Hamlet*: 'There is nothing either good or bad, but thinking makes it so'. Worry consists of our incessant fears that something has gone wrong. We are wired to worry. But whilst it may be inevitable, it is not always productive, certainly not when it becomes obsessive.

The way to reduce the worry is to stop, take a deep breath, and ask yourself whether this worrying is helping the situation. Are you simply trying to figure out the worst-case scenario in order to be prepared for every eventuality? Or are you working yourself into such a state where you can no longer function?

Worry is a form of visualisation, negative visualisation, where you envision all the things that might or will go wrong. Positive visualisation on the other hand is an excellent practice to stave off worry. Let us look at some situations and the difference between positively and negatively visualising the outcome can influence your thoughts.

Scenario: You have to make a major presentation at work, and a promotion you want is riding on it.

Negative visualisation: *This is going to be a disaster. I hate public speaking and this is worse because I know everyone in the audience. Not only will my boss be there but his boss too. Plus, the two people who are in line for this promotion will be there. They're going to see me blowing this and laugh. If I blow this chance, I might even lose my job…*

Positive visualisation: *OK, I'm nervous but everyone gets performance anxiety. My boss wouldn't have asked me to make this presentation to his boss if he didn't have a lot of confidence in me. I'm going to get up there and do great. I don't have to be perfect! If I'm relaxed and enjoying myself, the audience is going to relax too. I can do this. I see myself at the podium, fully prepared, answering their questions knowledgeably and they're all nodding in approval. It's going to be terrific!*

Positive visualisation allows you to imagine how things will be if everything that happens is the best possible outcome. Your brain starts to get re-wired for greatness and you start to take action. It is the law of attraction again. Visualisation can be empowering.

As humans, we put ourselves under a lot of stress. It is helpful to identify what triggers stress in us so that we can prepare for these circumstances, visualise things turning out well, and remind ourselves that life is not perfect and neither are we.

Does your stress stem from a deep-seated feeling that you are not good enough? If so, try positively visualising what changes you can make that would make you feel better about yourself. If you are worried about your weight, or you do not like your job, these are all things that can be fixed. You can diet and exercise and get a new job. Simplicity in identification is the key.

Take responsibility for your own thoughts. Being more conscious of how you think and feel provides you with more control in your life. Solutions to what may have been difficult problems present themselves more readily.

Ego and self-image

Often, our fears of what other people think of us lie at the root of the stress we feel. You only need to impress and be honest with yourself. The good people around you will accept you, no matter what you do.

We all make choices. We have the ability to get out of the choices, or massage or manipulate them, or move forward with them. Stress comes with responsibility. Work with what you've got and what you set out to do. If you cannot, then change direction.

Mindfulness

Mindfulness is about anchoring yourself in the present moment, ignoring the past and not thinking about the future, merely stepping out and observing yourself with no judgement or critical way of thinking, just viewing.

You go shopping and get in line to check your goods. What is the checkout lady doing? What colour hair does the person in front of you have? Do you have a smile on your face?

You can practise mindfulness for several moments throughout the day. Once you start doing it, you will be startled how much you have missed up until now. We are unaware most of the time exactly what it is we are doing when we are doing it because our minds are elsewhere.

How many times have you forgotten your keys or your phone, only to find them in your hand or right in front of you? How many times have you spoken to someone, then forgotten what you said or did? You are thinking of a million different things whilst doing one thing.

Practising mindfulness enables us to become more conscious. This dramatically increases our consciousness of what we are doing and how we are, daily. Pause and think of yourself for two to three minutes, repeat your name and think of just you. You will find that you will stop suddenly, because it does not feel natural and real. This has to be practised regularly. You will become more mindful and you will find yourself become so much calmer and rational in life.

After you have had an outburst or tantrum, you need to replay it in your mind like you are watching a TV show episode. Pretend that you are an actor, see what you looked like, how you felt and appeared, watch your thoughts, etc. You may have thoughts like: why was that person so rude? You essentially watch your own movie and you do not cast any judgement on it. You just observe.

When you watch everything from a third person point of view, you no longer bond with the pain, suffering, and emotions. This means that you do not overreact. Mindfulness can be the one tool that stops people from drowning their sorrows in escapes like booze and drugs because they learn to cope. You do not need to drown; you can swim freely.

Alternatives

Listening to relaxing music has been shown to decrease blood pressure, heart rate, and anxiety levels in heart patients. Pets also lower stress spikes in their owners' blood pressure as compared to those who do not own pets. Having a sense of humour is recommended by stress management experts. Laughter releases tension from built-up feelings, helps get things in perspective, and reduces stress hormone levels.[29]

Journaling can be a powerful way to address the stress blockage. Try writing down your innermost viewpoints and feelings to help put things into perspective. It can also help you feel more in control and promotes a positive outlook.

'Chunking-down' is another method to alleviate stress. Break big problems down into smaller parts, which makes the overall problem seem more manageable. Shrink things, make everything smaller, and just breathe. (I find this strategy particularly effective.)

SUMMARY

- Stress is increasing in today's fast-paced world, more than doubling in the last 40 years.

- The stress blockage interrupts goal achievement.

- People with the stress blockage tend not to make good decisions and feel perpetually exhausted.

- Research shows that short-term stress leads to better performance, but chronic stress can harm your health.

- To reduce worry, stop, and ask yourself if the worry is helping you.

- Mindfulness is an effective stress reliever.

Blockage 9: The Relationship Blockage

> *When one door of happiness closes, another opens, but often we look so long at the closed door that we do not see the one which has been opened for us.*
>
> Helen Keller

As humans, we place a high value upon relationships. We tend to believe relationships should always be wonderful, fulfilling, and bring us joy and happiness. We are social animals. We love talking and communicating with others, and these interactions generally shape our happiness. Studies have shown that solid, positive relationships increase lifespan and improve health.[30]

When two people become involved in an intimate relationship, they experience a warm and fuzzy feeling caused by the release of dopamine, the body's 'feel-good' hormone. Dopamine helps us to pay attention, take risks, experience elation, and be adventurous. Dopamine effects can last hours, days, and even weeks.

Unfortunately, experiencing this brain chemistry when we are in love does not necessarily mean we will end up having a successful relationship. According to Arthur Aron, a psychologist who studies love, 'Those who are intensely in love from the outset are only slightly more likely to have a good relationship'.[31] The final outcome will likely depend upon the way a person feels about themselves and the way they relate to their partner.

People with the relationship blockage may feel incomplete, uncomfortable being self-reliant, and therefore searching for someone to complete them. Romantic ballads notwithstanding, this is not a healthy perspective. These stuckburies consist of painful feelings, fears and doubts about whether someone can meet their own needs, hoping instead that someone else can do it for them.

People with the relationship blockage replay their emotional issues from their childhood in their current relationship, when parents fail to give their children the confidence they need to stand on their own. The parents do everything for them, and the child never learns there is a limit to what other people can provide. Ultimately, they never learn how to meet their own needs.

The relationship blockage can also develop where a child feels that they are not acknowledged or appreciated. When they experience repeated rejection, they learn to cope by numbing themselves to the hurt and become afraid to rely on others for fear of experiencing that pain anew. They may even develop a rather sophisticated fantasy life, sensing there is greater safety there and in retreating from others.[32]

As adults, they may feel worthless, having been criticised and rejected by their parents, and so they fear the risk of pain in real interactions. They are scared they will be hurt again. If, in fact, they do find someone who loves them, they become suspicious of their partner, even attacking them for being loving, because the partner's image of them does not reflect how they feel about themselves, namely unworthy of love.[33]

Living example of a relationship blockage

Miles was a successful sales representative in the real estate industry. He dreamed of becoming a manager, however, after 15 years, he still had not made this a reality. He was known for his nice clothes, car, and his great sales ability. Miles would outperform the other salespeople but yet he never got promoted. He resented others who had secured positions of authority.

As a child, Miles always got what he wanted. As an adult, he continued thinking that he could get other people to do what he wanted. When someone told him what to do, he resented it. Miles' stuckbury was authority. It was getting in the way of his relationships with others, and his ability to succeed.

People with the relationship blockage live in fear they will not be able to get what they need from their partner. They attempt to resolve this by trying to influence or control the other person by withdrawing, being jealous, blaming, lashing out, manipulating, withholding, and lying.[34]

By resolving a relationship stuckbury, you experience your life in new and different ways. Otherwise, they will continue to resurface, replaying the same old issues in each new situation.

Living example of a relationship blockage

Richie had always been a bit pudgy as a child and was self-conscious about it. His classmates pounced on his lack of self-confidence and frequently teased him. As a result, he withdrew into himself. He had few friends.

One day one of the more popular girls at school had a fight with her boyfriend. Allison stood in the near-empty hallway, her face red with anger. She whirled around and spotted Richie nearby, watching them. Embarrassed, he turned away and was startled when he felt her take his arm. 'Who needs him?' she said, giving Richie a flirtatious smile. She smirked at Tom before turning back to Richie. 'Walk me to my class, won't you?' Richie stared at her before breaking into a huge grin. 'Sure!'

That afternoon he told his friends and parents excitedly that he had a girlfriend and how popular she was.

The next day, Richie wrote on the school wall, in big letters, in bright yellow chalk, *Richie loves Allison*. The other kids jeered at him. Stung, Richie cried out, 'She likes me too. Just ask her!' He turned and spotted Allison standing next to Tom and some of her friends. 'Tell them!' Richie cried. She laughed. 'Don't be silly, fat boy! Who would like you?'

Richie was devastated. He found it extremely hard to trust anyone after that. Even after he shot up in height and slimmed down, he found it impossible to approach women whom he found attractive. If a woman approached him, he was always suspicious of her motives, questioning why she would choose him and convinced she would disappoint.

Children can be affected when they are brought up in families where the parents are not connected. They see relationships as being clouded by the coldness or the lack of connection.

When a child has not experienced a healthy loving parental connection, they are unfamiliar with how to act in a healthy relationship. They do not know how a relationship should be, to extract the best out of each partner. Intimacy and warmth can be difficult to display and accept.

Similarly, children brought up in an aggressive, addiction-based parenting situation learn to associate their emotions and committing to someone else as risky and not worth the hurt. They get scared that, by committing, they will get hurt.

Alternatively, they might mimic their parents' behaviour by becoming aggressive or indulging in substance abuse. Many times, they isolate themselves to avoid the abuse and aggression they associate with their parents. They have trust issues.

Techniques to unblock

There are various things that can be done to address phobias centred on commitment. Communication, while challenging, is a good place to start. Choose someone you trust, like a close friend. If you have trust issues with your partner, it is easier to take small steps and start working your way up the ladder to your partner. Roughly 55 per cent of communication is visual body language and eye contact, 38 per cent is tone of voice, and the words you use make up only 7 per cent.[35] The smallest movements, stances, and techniques make all the difference.

To have a healthy relationship, you need to have the right focus. If your focus is skewed by your emotional baggage, then you are setting yourself up for disaster. If you have stuckburies, and you are not doing anything about the blockages, you instead look for someone who reinforces your blockages. Due to the law of attraction – that like attracts like – you may inadvertently attract someone suffering from a similar blockage.

Relationships are challenging – no relationship is smooth all the time. They challenge us to see our weaknesses and (hopefully) do something about them. Relationships are all about partners working together to fix things. To sustain a relationship takes lots of work, dedication, and sacrifice.

Author and speaker Stephen Covey cites three types of relationships: co-dependent, independent, and interdependent.

Co-dependent relationships are the most damaging. Co-dependency is where two people come together because each person fills the other's needs. For example, Jenny is insecure whilst Brian is over-confident. Jenny is attracted to Brian's extreme confidence whilst Jenny's meekness satisfies Brian's need to feel in charge. They feed off each other instead of bringing out each other's best.

Independent relationships are where two people are totally self-reliant. Whilst self-reliance is a good thing, too much independence in a relationship prevents bonding. In an independent relationship, each person puts themselves first, and an absence of nurturing and of coming together may result.

Interdependent relationships, Covey says, are the ideal relationships, one where you work with your partner for the betterment of both. It is about cooperation and a common goal. So, you may be interdependent, but you also want to grow and bond together. Each partner is self-reliant in a healthy way, without a fear of connection or using the other person to fulfil an emotional void. Interdependence is about achieving a balance between giving and taking, between self-reliance and support.[36]

Healthy people, as I pointed out earlier, attract healthy people. People are naturally drawn to powerful and confident people. Learning to be happy and content on your own is important, and it is a lot easier to say than do. It is about acting 'as if', adopting behaviours that reflect the kind of person you want to be.

Now, if you wanted to lose weight, you would exercise and make healthier food and drink choices. You would be acting like someone who's fitness-minded, doing the things that fitness-minded people do. The same process applies to things like being more confident. You take a deep breath, visualise how confident people behave and see yourself behaving the same way, and then doing it, without seeking confirmation from others that your decisions are the right ones, without giving in to the fear of not wanting to try something new in case it fails – taking a chance and asking someone you like to join you for a cup of coffee.

As you practise, it becomes easier. As you practise more and more, you grow to like yourself more and more, to the point where you welcome time alone because you enjoy your own company. Ask yourself, why would anyone want to be alone with you if you don't like being alone with you? The goal here is to become healthier and more independent so as to be able to achieve true interdependence.

Here are some things you can do to build healthier relationships:

Take an interest – This does not mean that you need to immerse yourself in someone else. It means that you need to give them some of your time and attention. It is about being mindful of them, being courteous and respectful. And that means switching off phones, electronic items, and other petty distractions and making time to enjoy each other's company.

Show your appreciation – Forget the infrequent grand gestures and focus on the little things to bolster your relationship. Small, consistent acts of thoughtfulness strengthen a relationship far more than a single expensive gift every year on a birthday.

Listening – Being a good listener is often the greatest gift you can give someone. Be attentive to their feelings and worries. Talk less, listen more, and avoid interrupting. Psychologists do a great job focusing on and listening to their clients. Few things are as important to another human being than the sense of being heard.

Be a best friend – Being a great partner in a loving personal relationship is about being a wonderful friend. It is not just about loving; it is about liking. Friendship can hold relationships together when times get tough. When you are friends you can communicate openly and honestly.

Laughter – Laughter, genuine joyous laughter, is infectious. And a shared laugh brings you closer to someone than shared misery. Find things you can laugh about together to bring you closer.

Avoid competing – Reluctance to compromise, and being intent on winning at every turn, destines you to failure, over and over again. If you continually win, you are in fact losing. You need to learn to willingly compromise. Once you respect what your partner needs, you are much more likely to have your needs met.

Get yourself right – Before trying to change your relationship dynamics, you need to validate yourself first. Assess yourself and your life position to determine whether you are happy and what you might need in order to be happy. If you are not on track to where you want to be in life, then you cannot help anyone else.

Addressing conflict – Avoid being reactive, as it causes us to say and do things we regret. Instead of lashing out, think of that childhood admonition to stop and count to ten. The idea is to pause and collect yourself before reacting in haste. By addressing and seeing things fairly, you will resolve situations more quickly. Resist the temptation to drag issues and arguments from the past into the mix. All that does is prevent you from forgiving, which is a negative state of mind. Both parties need to feel that they have been heard and appreciated with respect.

Physical contact – Affectionate touching, whether it is intimate, such as hugging, hand-holding, or sex, or simply friendly contact, like touching someone's arm, creates a feeling of connection and helps bond us to others. When we experience positive physical contact, our bodies release the hormone oxytocin, which makes us more sympathetic, supportive, and open to others.

Expect ups and downs – You will not always agree. Accept that. Different people cope with stress differently. Interpretations can quickly turn to frustration and anger. Measuring the coping ability under stress is important. Some days you will cope better than on others.

Give and take – Healthy relationships are built on give and take. You cannot expect to get what you want all the time, and if you do, you likely won't feel as satisfied as you think you will. The strongest relationships are built on compromise and both parties need to give as well as take.

Avoid taking people for granted – Remembering to regularly stop and think about what you are grateful for, particularly in the other person, helps to keep affection and regard alive. It is easy to get caught up in the day-to-day routines and put activities ahead of people. That is a mistake. Consider taking just a few minutes each day, when you wake up, to tick off the things you are grateful for, including your partner. It is a great way to put you in a positive frame of mind to face the day.

Get out there – My favourite way to increase my friend network is to solicit meeting the friends of those I admire most. Be open to social media. Online groups like meetup.com host great ways to meet people. Find volunteer activities that align with your interests. If you are an active hiker, volunteer as a guide. If you like to cook, consider working a few hours a week in a soup kitchen. You get the idea. Do not count on your partner to entertain you. A healthy relationship is where individuals have the space to pursue their own interests as well as share time together.

Be honest and upfront – I am a firm believer in transparency. Keeping secrets from your partner breeds distrust. The most important tool we will have in a relationship is trust. Once lost, it can sometimes prove impossible to regain.

Do not try to 'fix' people – Accepting a person for who they are is one of the greatest gifts you can give them. People with the relationship blockage are often guilty of trying to change their partner to suit their needs. This comes from their fear they cannot otherwise get what they think they need. If you catch yourself doing this, try taking responsibility for meeting your own needs.

It is important to feel safe in communicating fears to your partner and for them to feel comfortable communicating theirs to you.

No one appreciates having their fears and concerns, no matter how seemingly insignificant, belittled or dismissed. Think of the ideal interdependent relationship. You want to work together to create a safe, loving environment in which to thrive.

In sales and corporate life, I gauge my success on the quality of the relationships I build, the rapport and trust that I work hard to create. People value honesty and a willingness to help. It always amazes me how many people are not willing to provide this anymore. Businesses are built upon relationships and having a happy, productive workforce with a clear mission, vision, and values.

SUMMARY

- A fear of intimacy develops when children feel unseen or misunderstood and grow into adults who are not confident in their own self-worth. People with the relationship blockage relive their childhood emotional issues in their adult relationships.

- People with relationship blockage expect other people to meet their needs for them.

- There are three types of relationships: co-dependent, independent and interdependent. The healthiest relationships are interdependent relationships where partners maintain their individuality whilst supporting each other.

Blockage 10: The Struggle Blockage

> *If you can't fly then run, if you can't run then walk, if you can't walk then crawl, but whatever you do you have to keep moving forward.*
>
> Martin Luther King, Jr.

The struggle blockage stems from a fear of criticism and lack of confidence.

Children who grow up in an environment where making mistakes is unacceptable and the parents focus only on what they do wrong, and ignore or take for granted what they do right, can find themselves all but paralysed in adult life when faced with having to put themselves on the front line in order to do anything. They fear trying to do their best at something and coming up short.

Accordingly, they avoid making decisions or trying to succeed for fear of failure and having to endure the criticism they are convinced will follow. They prefer to play a supporting role where they do not have to extend themselves too much.[37]

Living example of a struggle blockage

Darryl is a shipping clerk at a major shipping company. He is reliable and steady, methodical and conscientious in his work. He finds comfort in the repetition and routine. His manager would like to promote him to a more senior role, but whilst Darryl would love to earn more money and be rewarded for his efforts, he's unsure he's ready to assume greater responsibility. He fears he will lose the ease in which he does his current job and disappoint his boss. He is not convinced the new position is a risk worth taking.

As a child, he was often the target of his mother's incessant criticism and volatile moods. She pounced when he did anything, quick to find fault, and ignored his achievements or scoffed at them. He quickly learned to keep a low profile and not do anything that might irritate her or bring her wrath down upon him. Convinced that he was mediocre, he avoided sports and all forms of competition, loath to put himself out there to be criticised.

Darryl associates trying new things with criticism, preferring tasks and responsibilities that are not overly challenging. He is convinced that he lacks what it takes to succeed or impress anyone.

Similarly, children whose parents praise them for things they have not achieved, or abilities they do not have, may fail to develop a healthy sense of self-esteem. Instead of self-confidence, they develop self-importance, an inflated sense of how important and talented they are. They are confused when confronted by their limitations and find ways to avoid revealing their inadequacies by avoiding responsibility.[38]

They cloak themselves in perfectionism, assuring everyone (and themselves) that their projects need just that little bit more work to be perfect before putting them out there. They dream of fantastic success but find excuses as to why they have not yet achieved it, content to have that dream of success just out of reach at all times.

People with this blockage get bogged down in trivial details, unable to focus on what is important. They continually sabotage their own efforts and are stuck in the struggle blockage. They find it easier to fail than to make an effort to succeed.

People caught in the struggle blockage sabotage things in their lives so that they end up struggling, or they introduce something into their life that takes a lot of time and energy whilst making little or no difference. It keeps them busy going nowhere, and they have no time to do anything else.

They make life difficult for themselves by obsessing about things that, in the scheme of things, do not matter. Instead of putting their time and energy into the things that do matter, they sabotage their own success. They do this because they believe deep down that they are unlikely to ever achieve the kind of success they secretly dream about.

Living example of a struggle blockage

Peter worked as a public servant and could often be heard fretting about his job, the system, the government, and employment conditions. He would invariably get caught up in unimportant tasks and little details, obsessing that everything had to be perfect.

Meanwhile, he started a landscaping side business, with the goal being to get the business to a level where he could leave his regular job. He went with a franchise arrangement that would provide him with leads to quote on and sell. Peter was a good salesperson and tradesman, and the landscape business quickly took off to the point where he needed to hire a couple of subcontractors, take a leave of absence, or resign. He did none of these things, and after only five months, gave up his landscape business.

Would you have done what Peter did? Facing up to what is important can be uncomfortable for people. Failing is familiar and does not involve change, which they might not how to cope with. If they succeed, new responsibilities may come along with it, which can be intimidating. People might expect them to succeed again, and if they cannot, they fear letting people down. Success is also recognised by others, and these blockage sufferers fear being in the spotlight.

People with the struggle blockage fear who they will become and how others will relate to them if they succeed. They get used to their existing place in society; it is a large part of who they are. If they succeed, they fear losing their identity. People grow accustomed to their position in relation to their peers, and success can change these relationships. They worry that people who were once their equals may begin to view them differently, possibly resentfully or enviously.

Success changes the way people feel about themselves. If people do not have a high regard for themselves, success conflicts with their sense of self. Failure is more in in line with their self-beliefs. If they do succeed, they chalk it up to a lucky break. They believe that success was undeserved in order to maintain their more comfortable low opinion of themselves.

In a study on achievement by Niiya, Brook, and Crocker, published by the journal *Self and Identity* in 2010, achievement was important to one group of participants and was directly correlated to how much effort they put in. The second group also believed that achievement was important but felt that their ability to achieve was fixed, not guaranteed if they invested a high level of effort.

The participants were asked to choose and listen to a piece of music whilst completing a task. The music was presented as either performance enhancing or detracting. The participants who believed achievement was related to effort tended to choose the music identified as hindering performance. They also chose to skip any practice questions before taking a test.

The researchers concluded that the participants who felt their level of effort marked their potential for success were in fact subconsciously sabotaging their performance, so that they could blame any subpar performance on the music or having skipped the practice questions.[39]

Techniques to unblock

If a person is stuck in the struggle blockage and fears success because they are scared of the unknown, they could work out what the possible outcomes could be if they succeeded. They could consider how they would feel about themselves, how their life might change, and how others would feel towards them. By doing this, they could familiarise themselves with what could happen, and adjust to any changes that might arise. Working out what will happen as a result of success might help lessen their fear, as the outcomes are no longer unknown.[40]

Another way to deal with the struggle blockage is to consider what help might be needed to deal with change. This could involve joining a group of people with the same goal or interest, sharing aspirations with good friends, or reading a book about striving for something new in life.

As we saw in the Part 1, Stuckburies, we are born with eight emotions wired into our heads. All other emotions are a combination of these eight primary emotions: sadness, happiness, fear, surprise, anger, shame, disgust, and interest/anticipation.

When we are in the struggle blockage, we feel urged to do something in response to these emotions. For example, if you are bored with life, you may start stressing and worrying about insignificant things, and before you know it, you find yourself struggling.

Sometimes, the smallest trigger can bring up these feelings of confusion from the past and make people angry or irritable. Ask yourself what kicked off your feeling helpless and out of control. Did it resemble anything from your past? To uncover the source of these feelings requires significant soul searching and the willingness to be brutally honest with yourself.

By observing and analysing your emotions, you become more in tune with what causes you to feel the struggle that you do. Let's look at how you might tackle this. I have included two samples to guide you in completing this exercise. Start with the first emotion, sadness, when you analyse how you react to certain situations.

The struggle blockage is fear based. It is you fighting against life. When you swap things like expectation for acceptance, you worry less about what you think other people expect of you. Accept that if you do your best, and accept it as your best, fearing an inability to meet others' expectations goes out the window. Struggling can generate indecisiveness, but if you have the right intention, then no matter how you look at things, you can back yourself and the journey.

With the correct focus, things tend to work out for the better. For example, if you buy a plant and focusing on the positive, watering and nurturing it, it will grow, whereas if you simply focus on acquiring plants but neglect their care, they eventually wither and die.

Description Assessment and Improvement of Emotions

Emotion	Rate 0 to 10 for strength	What stories negatively affect your emotions?	(a) What do you feel physically? (b) How do you think you look to outsiders?
Sadness	7	I doubt my ability to succeed in my career	(a) When I think about this, I feel tired, overwhelmed. (b) My eyes are dull and my face downcast or expressionless.
Happiness	6	I feel happy when my partner is a bit off-balance and feeling insecure.	(a) It makes me feel more in control. (b) I look smug and self-satisfied.
Fear			(a) (b)
Surprise			(a) (b)
Anger			(a) (b)
Shame			(a) (b)
Disgust			(a) (b)
Interest / anticipation			(a) (b)

(a) What do you feel like doing when you feel this emotion? (b) Will it favour you if you do this?	(a) What is a better behaviour you can use? (b) Would another behaviour improve how you feel?
(a) I feel an urge to call my parents / best friend. (b) No – when I do this I am behaving in a co-dependent way, which prevents me from developing confidence.	(a) I can go for a walk / meditate to music I have on my smartphone that's designed to increase positive vibes. I can remind myself of, and appreciate, what I have achieved in my career so far. And I can review my goals and start focusing more on them. (b) These new behaviours will improve how I feel about myself, give me more energy, and likely improve my posture and appearance.
(a) I feel like giving her advice. (b) No, this makes me come across like a bully.	(a) I can change the subject so that she gets distracted and learns to combat things on her own so she gets stronger emotionally. (b) Yes, I would feel more kindly towards her and ideally make her feel the same, so we can relax and enjoy each other more.
(a) (b)	
(a) (b)	
(a) (b)	
(a) (b)	
(a) (b)	
(a) (b)	

Being mindful

When we are in the struggle blockage, we are not living in the present. When we accept and feel the present, we can more readily positively impact our problems. By focusing on what we have and where we are at this moment in time, the brain cannot focus on either the past or future.

The more we are present, the more we become distracted from struggle. This is why meditation is so powerful. It forces you to stop and feel the now. Your creativity will start to expose itself, quietly and frequently. You encounter the joys of being present because you do not have as many distractions. Distractions stop you from opening up and finding and sourcing great ideas and methodologies.

Possible solutions

Humour, your ability to laugh and see the funny side of things, can be your best friend when caught in the struggle blockage. Laughter really can be the best medicine, helping you to relax and alter your perspective from one that is too black and white.

Shifting your perception is also helpful. If, for example, you are someone who struggles with a fear of success, convinced that you are being scrutinised by others, try imagining the opposite scenario, if roles were reversed. If a person you feel is scrutinising you does something well, would you applaud or criticise? Healthy people know that someone else's success does not affect them negatively. If a person is critical of you when you do a good job, their negativity has more to do with themselves and their character than with your performance.

A person who is frightened of finding out that their efforts are not enough can start by setting small goals that present a challenge but are not overwhelming. Achieving small goals helps to boost confidence, illustrating that they are good enough to do something well. For example, if a person wants to gain a new qualification, they could start by making enquiries about the course and researching it on the internet. By succeeding in these smaller steps, the person will feel more confident in taking the next step.[41]

Many attempts to succeed are not necessarily touchdowns, but a willingness to try and to keep trying. However, perseverance is not the same as spending too much time perfecting one or a few attempts; this is the surest way to fail. Thomas Edison said it best when he said that the definition of insanity is doing the same thing over and over again and expecting different results. If your efforts do not resolve a problem, then you need to be creative and approach the problem from different angles. A few failed attempts are not confirmation of a person's inadequacy or that they do not deserve to succeed.

Living example of a struggle blockage

Sandra is a writer who loves her job. Her boss is an energetic man who likes getting things done. He likes her enthusiasm, however he finds she gets bogged down when researching her subjects. He tells her that timelines are important and suggests she spend less time researching in order to meet those timelines. Sandra gets paid daily, so the excessive time spent researching is costing the company.

Sandra's boss decides to pay her by the project. After a few weeks, Sandra realises that to make more, she needs to spend less time researching and focus on doing each job as well as she can in the time allotted. Once she does, the quality of her work improves because, rather than getting caught up in detail, she is now looking at the bigger picture. The result? Both she and her boss are happier.

SUMMARY

- The struggle blockage is when people sabotage their efforts because they are afraid of what will happen if they succeed. They bog themselves down in the trivial, at the expense of what is important.

- Where children grow up in an environment where the focus is only on what they do wrong, they become self-critical and are afraid to push beyond their comfort zone to succeed.

- Children who are rewarded for things they have not achieved, or abilities they do not possess, fail to develop a healthy sense of self-esteem. Instead of developing self-confidence, they develop self-importance, which hinders their ability to succeed in later life.

- Struggle can be an addictive state of mind where people perceive struggling over what's unimportant as accomplishment. Some subconsciously self-sabotage to avoid discovering whether they can do a good job.

- By doing our best and accepting it, we fear less the expectations of others.

PART 3
Learning to Stay Successful
The 10 Principles to Stay Successful

Principle 1: The Crystal Clear Principle

> *Efforts and courage are not enough without purpose and direction.*
>
> John F. Kennedy

Have you ever worked hard yet felt you were no closer to success? Do others make headway whilst you get left behind? The answer may lie in whether you possess a clear direction and focus. When you have a clear direction that aligns with your goals, it is likely your aspirations will become a reality. But for many, the prospect of getting what they want is scary. It is all too easy to get sidetracked by what is not important, as we saw in the last chapter, and overlook what is important. The inclination to veer away from what needs to be done and instead struggle with irrelevant detail stems more from a fear of success than fear of failure.

In Blockage 7, the shiny ball blockage, we examined how some people pursue one attractive opportunity after another, discarding each when distracted by the next opportunity, which appears more attractive because it is novel. They end up with a whole host of ideas, none of which are ever implemented. They lack clear direction and focus. By overcoming patterns that undermine success, a new world can be discovered, a world where there is clear direction and focus in the things we do. Everything just feels right in this world. To stay successful, it is important to keep on track. Staying successful is harder than initially achieving it.

Focus

Ever notice how, when you sit down to write something, the hardest part is getting started? Unless you are clear about exactly what you want to say, your mind flits from thought to thought, unsure of what approach to take.

According to Harvard psychologists Matthew A. Killingsworth and Daniel T. Gilbert, on average, people spend 46.9 per cent of their waking hours thinking about something other than what they are doing, and that this tends to make them unhappy.[42] People, they say, are far happier when they are consciously focused on something, whether that's conversation, intimacy, exercising or any other activity.

When we are in the present moment and being mindful, we can focus on one thing – our direction is clear. Many philosophical and religious traditions, such as Buddhism, believe that happiness is found by living in here and now versus letting thoughts of the past or fears of the future intrude.

Those successful in business and relationships experience ups and downs. What sets them apart is the way they deal with their inevitable changes in circumstance. Two individuals might have the same resources and skill sets. Whether they succeed or fail likely depends on how much focus and clear direction they possess.

If you feel rudderless, unsure of which way to go, stop and remind yourself of what it is you are trying to achieve and then decide what path you need to take to get there. If, for example, you and your partner discover you are expecting a child, that can create a new direction and purpose in your lives. In order to prepare, you might start reading books about raising children and readying yourself for a new arrival. If you fail to consciously prepare, you may find yourself overwhelmed with fearful thoughts of what lies ahead.

Living example of the Crystal Clear Principle

Philip was an entrepreneur and businessman who invested in various projects throughout his adult life. However, he would inevitably lose interest before any of his projects got off the ground. All that would remain was the debt he'd created, which would drive him to start yet another project.

At age 57, he sold his business, invested the proceeds, and made a substantial profit. It was the first time he had ever been debt-free. He purchased a home and a new car and took the family overseas. After a few months, he found himself in a deep depression, which baffled him because, generally speaking, he was finally successful. Instead of feeling buoyant about that, he felt hopeless and helpless. No longer with a goal in life, he felt stuck.

One afternoon, Philip twisted his ankle. He hobbled home but stumbled and fell down the stairs when his ankle gave way, causing him to rupture a disc in his spine and fracture his sprained ankle. Several operations ensued, requiring lengthy rehabilitation. When the therapy started, he focused on getting back on his feet and improving his health. Once recovered, he joined a gym and became a fitness buff.

Although Philip's accident was technically a setback, it served to launch him forward by giving him a concrete goal, a sense of purpose. His depression and lack of direction became a thing of the past.

Crystal clear direction is the ability to see where you are in life, where you want to go, and how you intend to get there. It is about focusing your attention on identifying and achieving your goals.

When we have destructive thoughts – that things won't work out or that we are not competent enough to succeed – we may be sabotaging our success because we fear what success might bring.

By focusing our attention on what is important, we can move forward with clear direction.

Confusion, or uncertainty in terms of direction, happens to the best of us. What separates the successful is their ability to gauge where their chosen path will take them, and if they do not like what they see, make corrections to their course. Facebook started with the simple premise to enable social networking among Harvard students, before expanding first to other colleges and then to the public at large. No one foresaw at its inception the global implications of such a site. YouTube's humble beginnings were as a dating site before burgeoning into a vast wellspring of video clips from entertainment to education and giving rise to countless entrepreneurial ventures.

Honing focus

When companies offer products and services with too many features, the focus and direction often becomes unclear. The message is too complex to be understood clearly. The focus of potential clients often gets confusing, and sales and productivity can be lost.

As Martin Zwilling wrote in his article, '6 Ways that Lack of Focus Can Kill Your Business,' on Forbes.com, marketing a product with too many features is almost impossible.[43] You cannot create a 'memorable message that has more than three bullets'.

Steve Jobs changed the way Apple operated by simplifying things, focusing on four products and targeting four markets. That continued focus survives Jobs and is directly responsible for Apple's continued success.

This same focus holds true for people. When we focus on too many things, we lack clear direction. We miss opportunities. We are less productive. A more razor-like focus enables us to move past distractions. The law of attraction, that like attracts like, says we attract that which we focus on, so the more we focus on a particular idea and the closer we draw to it, the more it becomes a part of our life.

Gratification

Adults who focus well were trained as children to finish things. As the adage goes, it is a lot easier to start something than to finish it. Why? Because the last 5 per cent takes about as much focus and energy as the first 95 per cent. People who stay focused are those who have learnt to delay gratification long enough to finish things. As children, it is natural to eagerly start something but not clean up the mess.

In the 1960s, Walter Mischel carried out what is called The Marshmallow Experiment. Children were given a marshmallow and left alone in a room for a short time after being told they could have a second marshmallow if they waited until the researcher returned to the room before eating the first one.

Some children wasted no time eating the marshmallow. Some struggled to wait but gave into temptation. And some children waited patiently until the researcher came back before taking it. Follow-up studies years later revealed that the children who delayed their gratification and waited for the second marshmallow were more successful in their achievements, such as higher scholastic assessment test (SAT) scores, lower likelihood of obesity, better responses to stress, and better social skills.

Having a clear direction and focus means having fewer distractions. If you focus on the negative, you won't be successful, but if you focus on the positive, you can achieve success. Learning to say no more often lessens the number of decisions you need to make. The fewer decisions you need to make, the fewer alternatives you need to consider and the less fatigued your brain will become. If you make fewer decisions and conserve your energy, you naturally focus better.

Losing focus

No one remains focused all the time without making mistakes and experiencing setbacks along the way. We are not talking about perfection here. You simply need to focus on the present, identify where you may have strayed from your desired path, and determine what you need to do to get yourself back on track again and do it.

Your brain will be better able to make good decisions if you minimise the number of decisions you need to make, and limit the number of alternatives. Maintain a healthy diet and get adequate sleep to keep your brain's store of energy at an optimal level. Focusing helps you to make better decisions, and prioritising those decisions keeps your brain functioning at its best, ensuring your direction is clear.

This is why it is important to set goals and work out the tasks that relate to those goals. When you delineate which tasks contribute to your goals, you are less likely to become distracted. If you do not set about accomplishing those related tasks, your goals may appear abstract and too difficult to achieve. For example, if your goal is to clean the house, it is not enough to simply decide you want to clean the house. You need to itemise what tasks will accomplish this. Is dusting and vacuuming enough or do you need to also mop floors? What about washing windows? Formulating the precise list of tasks necessary for you to accomplish what you set out to do is critical to success. You cannot navigate a boat without the necessary tools. Navigation is your goal; the tools are your tasks to accomplish the goal.

Mindfulness

People who pay attention to the present moment and the tasks at hand are more engaged in activities, get things done well, and deal with difficulties better. Having a clear focus enables people to achieve success. They are happier in life. People who are highly focused remove distractions that get in the way of doing a job well. Distractions increase the amount of stress people experience and decrease the ability to concentrate.

Distractions can come in the form of emails, social media notifications, or people who drop by to chat during work hours. Focused people do not indulge in procrastination. When they are tempted to put off something they think is difficult, they push themselves to get it done. People who are focused realise that the best time to do something is right now.

Our quality of life improves and our spirits lift when we redirect our focus from the negative to the positive. This is not about donning rose-coloured glasses and ignoring what needs fixing in our lives – it is about taking a positive approach to resolving the negatives and finding the positives in them so that rather than getting stuck in 'if-onlys' and regrets, we are solution-orientated and always focusing forward. If something feels particularly negative, jotting down a quick list of the things about it that you are grateful for can quickly reorientate your outlook.

When things go wrong

Once, in the space of a few hours, I went from everything going right to my mother being sick in hospital, my dog dying, and then my father being admitted to hospital. Suddenly my bright world appeared to be a dark place. I ended up ill myself, through lack of sleep and unhealthy eating.

When life and its challenges threaten to overwhelm, make it manageable by breaking down the problems into parts. Focus first on your goal, what it is you need to achieve (e.g., good health, meeting specific work deadlines, securing home health care for the ailing parent, etc.).

Second, prioritise these goals and break them down into the tasks necessary to achieve them. Avoid making critical decisions when your mind is gripped with fear, as we tend to act in haste (and often regret later). Don't dwell on what is going to happen if you don't solve the problem; focus only on the present – what steps you need to take to reach your desired goal. It is a bit like panicking when your car won't start and calling for a tow truck before taking a quick glance to see whether the battery is still connected and that you have sufficient petrol in the tank, or calling a repairman because the refrigerator has stopped working, only to have them hold up the power cord which had worked itself loose. Take a breath and go through your checklist instead of giving into helplessness and panic.

When we are under pressure, our perceptions get skewed. Picture this: I have to leave the house for an important meeting. I can't find my phone. I start to panic and I scream and shout, which raises my anxiety. I can't find my car keys, so I catch a cab. When I get home, I find the keys are in the ignition. I had been in such a hurry earlier that I unthinkingly left them there. High stress and emotional situations will invariably arise. Your focus needs to be on consciously slowing yourself down and having patience, with the knowledge that everything will be okay.

When we get bursts of adrenaline through our system due to fear, we can still focus. The adrenaline only lasts for a few minutes. Wait it out and then start analysing. The trick is to remain calm and keep your direction clear.

SUMMARY

- Children who learned to be patient and delay gratification are typically more successful later in life.

- When you lose focus and let your mind wander, more often than not it makes you feel unhappy as well as distracting you from succeeding.

- By reducing the number of decisions you make, your brain can more readily focus on what is important. If you have too many goals, your focus becomes divided and it is difficult to succeed.

- A clear sense of direction, in which you work out the tasks that directly relate to achieving your goals and set aside unimportant distractions, better enables you to achieve those goals.

Principle 2: The Dynamo Principle

> *If you're changing the world, you're working on important things. You're excited to get up in the morning.*
>
> Larry Page, CEO of Google

Have you noticed how truly successful people are upbeat and full of energy, hope, and ambition? Where does all this aspiration come from? They are charged with a positive focus, a strong desire, and ambition to reach their goals. Their visualisation so is strong that *they can mentally convert the things they want to the things they already have.*

Many of us tend to live our lives on automatic pilot, exerting no control over our thoughts, actions, or reactions. We are just along for the ride instead of taking the reins, going out and living our lives with purpose. Our mind wanders because we have not spent any time or effort establishing a sense of direction for ourselves. We are affected by the negativity around us. It draws our focus, eclipsing the positives. It is a hard cycle to break, and can affect us on many levels, as we learned in Blockage 5, with the negativity blockage.

Our mental and emotional states do not only impact our physical health – being positive open more doors. Carnegie-Mellon University psychologist Michael F. Scheier was cited in Daniel Goleman's 1987 *New York Times* article 'Research Affirms Power of Positive Thinking' as saying that 'optimists tend to respond to disappointments like being turned down for a job by formulating a plan of action and asking other people for help and advice; pessimists more often react to such difficulties by trying to forget the whole thing or assuming there is nothing they can do'. The article goes on to quote Christopher Peterson, a psychologist at the University of Michigan, who says that 'pessimists make a mess of their lives; more bad things befall them like break-ups, family troubles, and failure in school. They are also more lonely and estranged from people; talking gloom and doom is a turn off'. 'Optimism,' Goleman writes, 'can pay dividends as wide-ranging as health, longevity, job success and higher scores on achievement tests'.[44]

The Dynamo Principle is about having an optimistic outlook and a sense of purpose. The resulting positivity keeps you and others feeling energised, influenced, and inspired. For the Dynamo Principle to work, we must set the intention to generate an action that is *more* than what we normally would do. The continuous feedback loop between ambition, achievement, and optimism drives success. The Dynamo principle forces you to dramatically influence and help people.

By empowering ourselves with honesty and a sense of purpose, we set an ambitious path to commit to new actions. It can take the form of helping, or inspiring or teaching, others, or building or creating, for example.

Optimistic people are less likely to get swamped in a sea of negativity, and if they do, they do not stay there for long. Dynamic people tend not to get caught up in limiting beliefs; they stop the pattern before it becomes overwhelming. They ascribe to something that is bigger than they are.

Living example of the Dynamo Principle

Media powerhouse and philanthropist Oprah Winfrey founded the Oprah Winfrey Leadership Academy for Girls to provide educational and leadership opportunities for academically gifted girls in South Africa, girls ages twelve to thirteen who feature an 'I can' attitude and exhibit leadership qualities. All come from disadvantaged backgrounds.

'My own success has come from a strong background in reading and learning,' Winfrey says. 'The greatest gift you can give is the gift of learning. When you're changing a girl's life, it is not just that life. You start to affect a family, a community, a nation.'

Indicative of Winfrey's deep love of books, she made sure that wherever the girls walked, they had to pass the library, and she arranged for there to be plush seating around a welcoming fireplace, 'so the girls can read by the fire and spend time there with their friends'.

It was not a smooth path. Indeed, what started as a conversation in 2002 took five years, ending with the doors opening in 2007. Her ambition and desire to effect positive change in the world was the driving force behind realising her dream.

Stuckburies

It can be disempowering, even debilitating, to be stuck by blockages. When we free up our stuckburies, we need to stay in a positive upward spiral, as the brain can easily fall into previously wired patterns. Things may come up from the past and our default is to do what feels safe to avoid pain and discomfort. Having an open mind, we make decisions based on the present and the future, and use information from the past as a stepping-stone to change our thoughts. But thoughts are not necessarily reality.

In the book *Coming to Our Senses*, the founder of Mindfulness-Based Stress Reduction, Dr Jon Kabat-Zinn writes about how when we enter into true stillness, that it can eclipse our attention far more disturbingly than the external noise that surrounds us. He observes that we would likely be stunned by how much of our thinking is chaotic, narrow and repetitive; shaped by our past and our habits. Kabat-Zinn observes that we have no real appreciation or just how our thinking totally governs our lives. It is only by practising mindfulness and entering that stillness that we can break those patterns, see our thoughts for what they really are, and change how they influence how we live our lives.

Our behaviour is unconscious. By being more mindful, we can expose our learned behaviours and see the role they play in our lives.

Motivation

The Greek word *entelechy* was coined by Aristotle to define one's unique highest potential. Aristotle believed that everything on this planet possesses its own entelechy, a particular type of motivation, a need for self-determination, and inner strength directing life and growth to become all. Entelechy is a vital force that motivates and guides every living entity towards its highest self-fulfilment.

In order to reach our highest potential, we need a positive mindset. This enables us to work with the negative in a positive way, so the negativity becomes a propelling force in what we do.

Positivity is not a matter of being either positive or negative – it is about being positive *and* negative. We can't have up without down; there must always be balance in the universe. It is about finding a middle ground where you feel effective, optimistic and confident.

You need to be passionate about your dreams, disciplined, work hard, and have a clear direction. Success is all about challenging ourselves not necessarily to be the best, but to be the best we can be.

Successful people choose to be positive, even when things are not going well. They do not morbidly contemplate negative situations or sit around feeling sorry about their own situation. Instead they know there are positives to every situation, and that in every bad situation there is a phoenix waiting to rise from the ashes.

Change can be intimidating, stressful, even scary at times. That's where positivity and clear direction help. Focus on your passion for doing something, which serves as a terrific motivator. If you feel nervous or frightened by the prospect of change, examine closely, as objectively as you can, why you may be feeling scared. Being honest with yourself means getting your inner feelings out.

When I needed to learn how to write well, I gave myself a time frame. There was no need to spend forever perfecting it, I reminded myself. It wastes time and kills motivation. Think of it this way: you may aim for one thing, but if you do not get it, something else may come along that adds more value to your journey.

Momentum

Once you start learning, you feel better. Target dates are important in establishing a time frame. Each day, make two or more things happen to keep your vision alive. As long as you do something every day, the dream, the vision, and the journey will continue and gain momentum.

Having daily goals make you conscious of where you have progressed. Your dreams and vision are absolutely necessary to become successful. All you have do is to start.

You need to believe in yourself to keep motivation going. Everyone can be motivated when times are good, but when they are bad, that is when it is a challenge to continue to believe in ourselves. It is all about the way we interpret the situation.

The way to stay successful is to view difficulty as a challenge, an opportunity for growth, rather than a reason to give up. This builds resilience and stability. You do not need anyone to do this for you. Even when you are alone, you can resurface with a smile and a plan of attack. Remember, you are in total control of your thoughts.

Passion

What are you passionate about, and what do you have to change to achieve these passions? It starts with using your mind to change your brain. Thoughts are self-generated and when we learn to better manage our automatic, negative thoughts, we change and retrain our neural pathways.

Harvard professor and social psychologist Daniel Wegner, as explained in his classic book *White Bears and Other Unwanted Thoughts*, told study participants close their eyes and not think about a white bear.

After receiving those instructions, participants thought of the white bear more than once per minute. Wegner developed his theory of ironic processes, explaining why it is so hard to stop unwanted thoughts. When we consciously try not to think of something, one part of our mind works to avoid the thought, but another checks every now and then to make sure the thought is not coming up, and by doing that, brings the forbidden thought to mind.

This is why negative thoughts and painful memories play over and over in our heads. When we have them, the brain automatically continues this pattern. Yet, when we entertain positive thoughts, the brain performs the same repetition, continuing optimistic thoughts.

Changing thought patterns

Meditation requires quietening the mind and focusing only on the present, such as the breath as it goes in and out of the body. Thoughts and distractions invariably creep in, but as mindfulness teaches, the goal is to acknowledge the thought as existing and then release it and focus again on the present.

People who find it difficult to meditate have not yet learned how to quieten their minds. To start training the mind, one must change the thought processes from negative to positive. Positive thought patterns result in positive attitudes. These positive attitudes and thoughts provide clarity and calmness whilst negative thoughts interrupt inner peace. The two biggest distractors to the inner mind are stress and negative emotions.

During challenging times, we often look outward and blame our negativity on the person or thing causing our stress. Personal growth is better served by choosing to see other people's behaviours as reflections of the things you need to look at in yourself, like stuckburies – once we get to the root of our problems, we can deal with the emotions that cause our stress.

Our personal power comes from eliminating negative thoughts and diverting them to positive ones. The first step in doing this is awareness. Awareness is being conscious of your thoughts, without judgement. The more we observe what and how we think, the more consciously we can choose to interrupt these automatic patterns. Once you are consciously aware of your thoughts, you can redirect them, choosing and controlling where you want your thoughts to go.

Five inherent traits

Psychologists have identified five hard-wired traits:

1. Openness: how much (or how little) we enjoy adventure and new experiences.

2. Conscientiousness: how organised and dependable we are.

3. Extroversion: how sociable we are and how much we draw our energy from being around others.

4. Agreeableness: how trusting, helpful, and compassionate we are.

5. Neuroticism: how emotionally stable we are and how much or how little we worry about things.

The last one affects your outlook and optimism. It dictates how you react and respond to life's disappointments.[45]

When people get stressed, they lose their ability to laugh or see funny things. It is crucial to see the funny side to everything. This reminds you that you are not the most important person, that you are a person playing a part in a comedy of ups and downs. Laughing and being happy lowers blood pressure.

Taking yourself too seriously puts unnecessary pressure on you. Forget the 'You're only as good as your last month' sales philosophy. Replace it instead with, 'Enjoy the achieving, not the risk'. Risk is inevitable. When you place too much emphasis on risk, you subject yourself to more pressure than necessary. By learning to enjoy the process, not the outcome, and having fun, you can see the ups and downs for what they are.

Health is wealth

Part of the Dynamo Principle is staying energetic and charged for life. I am a firm believer in exercise.

Exercising should be a routine, like washing your hair or brushing your teeth. Research indicates that long hours spent working and too much work-related travel significantly increase feelings of unhappiness and lack of success. Recreation and socialisation is critical to one's wellbeing. We've become a sedentary society so it is more important than ever to get out and get moving. That also means eating and living better. Smoking, drinking, drugs, and an over-reliance on caffeine for energy have become unhealthy coping mechanisms.

SUMMARY

- The Dynamo Principle is the desire to achieve your unique highest potential, to discover your passions and put them into action to realise your purpose in life.

- The bigger you think, the greater the challenge, and the greater the challenge, the more exciting and purposeful your life becomes.

- Having an optimistic outlook and reducing limiting beliefs helps you stay in your personal power without getting stuck in negative patterns that overwhelm.

- With an open mind, we make decisions based on the present and the future, and use information from the past as a stepping-stone to change our thoughts.

Principle 3: The Purposeful Learning Principle

> *The only real mistake is the one from which we learn nothing.*
>
> — Henry Ford

Do successful people want to learn, need to learn, or naturally learn?

Peter Michael Senge, systems scientist, author of *The Fifth Discipline*, and founder of The Society for Organizational Learning, says that learning to do new things allows us to recreate ourselves, and that these new skills give us a new perspective on life. The idea is to link learning to a realistic purpose with attainable goals. Studies have linked performance to learning, particularly when there exists a passion for reading.

Problem-based learning is applying what you have learnt to solve problems effectively. It enhances your attitude towards what you learn and leads to a deeper approach to learning. Problem-based learning is self-directed, and learners develop life-long learning skills.

American psychologist Carl Rogers called experiential learning self-initiated learning; that is, people have a natural inclination to learn, become fully involved in the learning process, and have control over its nature and direction. 'Learning is most likely to occur and to last when it is self-initiated,' Rogers says.[46]

Purposeful Learning

The Purposeful Learning Principle is about linking and structuring our learning around our goals and purpose. Learning with the end in mind is paramount. Successful people are learning all the time. They learn to increase their performance based on what they think and, at the same time, they constantly assess where they are in relation to achieving their learning goals.

When we know what we want in life, we are more disciplined and invested in learning what we need to know to get it. We start by establishing a clear direction and focus, then set the necessary goals and tasks designed to take us there. When we know what our vision in life is, we can work out what we need to learn to realise it. When we learn in line with our goals, we develop and grow.

Embracing feedback

Successful people welcome feedback, negative and positive, as feedback helps them to gauge and better their performance. The more detailed and precise the feedback is, the better a person can identify what it is they need to do to improve.

There is a saying in sales that if you are a salesperson and your client provides little feedback after you make your sales pitch – that they need your product yet they need more time to think – then the deal won't go ahead. People who are interested will have questions and give feedback as an expression of their interest.

Successful people accept that they can always improve themselves. Many actively solicit feedback. Entrepreneur and philanthropist Bill Gates observed that 'Your most unhappy customers are your greatest source of learning'.

Practise, practise, practise

Practice makes perfect and learning is no exception. A whole host of little improvements come together as one big increase in knowledge. Learning basic skills like how to paint, drill, cut wood, join corners, and attach hinges potentially add up to one large accomplishment.

Incentives are the great motivator, whether they take the form of payment/bonuses, recognition, awards, etc. Reward yourself, however modestly, when you achieve milestones.

Develop your emotional intelligence quotient (EQ)

EQ is our ability to be sensitive and intuitive to the emotions of ourselves and others, and manage and express our own emotions. Emotional intelligence enables us to be more responsive, to build stronger relationships, and to improve happiness and life satisfaction levels, both in others and in ourselves.

High performers usually rate high in the intelligence quotient stakes. It is possible to increase one's EQ, mostly by being aware, thoughtful, and sensitive to what is going on around us. For example, you might:

- Find ways to manage your stress.

- Assume a friend who does not respond to an invitation has a good reason, rather than that they are being rude.

- Think first, rather than simply reacting.

- Not simply give in to situations; stand your ground where you feel it is appropriate to do so.

- Trust your feelings and try to understand them.

- Learn to express your emotions to those close to you.

Reading as part of purposeful learning

I was never much of a reader growing up, despite my mother's urging, but it was only in my professional life that I realised how much learning I had missed out on and how much catching up I had to do. For example, in sales meetings, it became starkly evident to me which people were well spoken, knowledgeable, and more interesting.

Without exception, the most articulate among us are passionate readers. One gentleman told me that he had not read since high school but began again at age 30. By the time he was 35 he was in a general manager position, whereas throughout his twenties, he had not been very successful. He told me that reading gave him undeniable power, not unlike the bullied child who learns to box. He developed a kind of aura, he told me, a confident presence that launched him forward.

Being well read brings many advantages, including speaking better, increased self-confidence, and being able to direct conversations. Reading can also be therapeutic and calms the mind as you focus on one thing, which limits distraction. Most successful people make time to read and read quality content on subjects that interest them and add value to their journey in life.

SUMMARY

- We need to link learning to a purpose that is realistic and attainable.

- Successful people learning constantly and assess where they are in relation to their learning goals.

- Lifelong learning is crucial to becoming an outstanding performer. If people do not keep learning, they don't stand still – they fall behind.

- Successful people welcome feedback, good and bad, and learn from it.

- If you are motivated by what you are learning, then you are likely to perform better. Motivation drives learning capacity and can increase self-confidence.

Principle 4: The SEV Principle: Select, Expect, Visualise

> *Opportunities don't happen.*
> *You create them.*
>
> Chris Grosser

How do you approach expectations? Do you expect the unexpected? Do you expect greatness? Do you lower your expectations to avoid being disappointed or hurt? You may think that maintaining low expectations will make you feel more balanced, but when we expect and focus on mediocrity, that is what lies ahead of us.

Expectations colour our perceptions of happiness and success. In the year 50AD, the philosopher Seneca noticed how those who were unhappy often had unrealistic expectations. Today we live in a world where, with all the advertising and social media, we are relentlessly compared to other people, usually in ways that attempt to make us feel as if we come up short.

Society seeks perfection in relationships, jobs, looks, and youth. We expect to be married forever, we decide we want children when our best friend has just had one and they look happy. Unrealistic expectations leave us feeling unfulfilled. But we can manage our expectations so they become more realistic.

- A 15-year-old girl is told not to walk through a particular neighbourhood at night because of its high crime rate. She does it anyway because she has no previous experience of harm, therefore no expectations of harm coming her way.

- A woman is dissatisfied with her job and leaves, only to take another in the same industry, as it is familiar. Should she anticipate similar dissatisfaction?

- You have just taken up skiing. You are so excited at making it off the beginner's slope that you envision yourself becoming a gold medallist at the next Winter Olympics. Is this realistic?

- If, instead, after taking up skiing, you fall and sprain your ankle during your first attempt, how would this experience colour your getting back up on your skis, if your expectation is now that you will inevitably get hurt again, perhaps even more seriously?

Visualisation

We build our expectations through the experiences we have, and how we feel or react to them, positive or negative. Expectations are our personal measuring posts, and by visualising, you can challenge your mind to find ways to reach your goals successfully. Feeling confident, strong, and positive about your goal drives you toward success. Negative thoughts sabotage success.

If visualisation, creating a mental image of a desired result, allows us to focus on things, and events, literally making things happen, as we saw with the Crystal Clear Principle, imagine how powerful a tool it can be in striving for success.

Shakti Gawain, author of *Creative Visualisation*, says that when you generate a strong intention to create something, it represents a deep desire. If you believe that you can do something and eagerly embrace it, it is likely to manifest it in your life in one way or another. He goes on to say that almost everything you truly need or want is here for the asking, you just have to believe it, desire it, and accept it.

Visualisation triggers the same physiological changes in the body as real experience. Imagine tasting cheesecake. Your brain prompts your salivary glands to respond to this anticipation in the same way as if the cake were in front of you.

Walt Disney said, 'If you can dream it, you can do it'. If you can visualise an outcome, you can plan a path to what you desire. Visualisation does not guarantee success, and does not replace planning and hard work; however, it can be a powerful tool to start the creative process to attain your goals. How often have you heard these words: 'You have the ability to achieve anything you put your mind to'?

Consider the placebo effect. In blind drug studies to test the efficacy of a new drug, one group of participants is given the medication and another a placebo, a substance that has no therapeutic value. Neither group knows who is getting the placebo and who is getting the real drug. Sometimes patients receiving the placebo exhibit a perceived or actual improvement in their medical condition, on occasion exceeding the results achieved by the real drug, illustrating the power of the mind in improving health indicators. The way that clinicians provide information to patients is thought to play a key role in the way patients respond to drug therapies.

Einstein declared that imagination is more important than knowledge, by which he meant that to imagine something opens doors to its realisation. Visualisation boosts self-confidence. When we 'see' ourselves winning, we are that much more likely to do so because of our increased self-belief. This is a well-known tactic in sports, used to increase concentration, drive, and coordination.

A young Irishman by the name of Conor McGregor, who was on social welfare, qualified to become a UFC (Ultimate Fighting Championship) fighter. A mere two years later he won a UFC world title, an incredible feat. McGregor spoke of how he constantly envisions living the life he strives for before he attains it, by using visualising his success.

SEV

SEV stands for Select, Expect, Visualise. It is about choosing a thought or goal, attaching a specific expectation to it, and then visualising it coming to fruition in a way that motivates you to actively pursue it and make it a reality.

This SEV Principle, the use of visualisation and belief in yourself combined with specific expectations, is a powerful tool to become and stay enthusiastic, motivated, and successful.

Creative visualisation is also an effective healing tool. It goes straight to the source of the problem: your mental concepts and images. As Shakti Gawain states in her book *Creative Visualisation*, 'Our personal experiences help shape our expectations over time. As we navigate the ups and downs of our decisions, we learn where we are placing too-high or too-low expectations on ourselves and can modify our thinking'.

How expectations originate

When our mothers were pregnant with us, they were said to be 'expecting'. When we are born, we are expected to arrive on a certain date. Our parents have expectations that we will be happy, healthy, and have a better life than they did. We are expected to graduate high school, perhaps go to university, get a good job, take care of our family. We learn from family and friends that we either want to be the same, better, or not like them, depending on our own perceptions.

We are exposed via TV and social media to things we could or 'should' have. Our cultural differences put expectations on us. We either sit comfortably or uncomfortably along these spectrums, depending on whether we think we are meeting our own or others' expectations.

It is common for people to feel pressure to achieve, behave, or look a certain way. These expectations can be positive, challenging or motivating us to do our best. Creating too many unrealistic expectations, however, can have a negative impact on our thoughts, feelings, and behaviour. Expectations can elevate us when they are on track, but if they go wrong, they can disappoint and hurt. If we select and define our expectations, we can control our path to success without feeling like we are on a rollercoaster.

Living example of the SEV Principle

When Janine hired Suzanne, Suzanne was confident and vibrant, and seemed perfect for the job. Janine's expectations were that Suzanne would work efficiently and help her to better manage the company. Suzanne assured her that she shared these expectations, but Suzanne had difficulty seeing tasks through to completion, failing to visualise the desired outcome. Suzanne was capable, but lacked direction and struggled to achieve her potential. After two months, Janine had no choice but to let Suzanne go.

Managers in the corporate world set increasingly high expectations and goals because they think it motivates staff. If every time you approach a target or goal it gets yanked out of reach, the repeated lack of reward and rise in expectations will demotivate you. If goals are unrealistic and unattainable, performance decreases due to lack of enthusiasm. Setting achievable goals and having incentives along the way is what keeps people motivated.

There are two types of visualisation, outcome visualisation and process visualisation, and they should be used together. Outcome visualisation, where you envision the outcome, is where you see yourself achieving your goal. You use all of your senses to create a detailed mental image of succeeding and attaining your goal, for instance, standing at the podium, holding the prize.

Process visualisation is where you imagine what's involved in the process necessary to achieve the outcome: the tasks or steps required to get to the target.

When we select our thoughts and expectations, it is vital to use common sense so we are not left managing unattainable or ridiculous expectations. With effective expectations it may seem that you can navigate your life in a positive direction. By believing in your abilities and managing your expectations, people may feel naturally drawn to you because of your enthusiasm and excitement.

The more we positively visualise something, the more likely we are to achieve it. The same goes for a desired behaviour. If, for example, we want to be more outgoing, we visualise being that way in various social situations, and envision being successful by thinking about what steps we should take to achieve it. That enables us to put it into practice, feeling more confident about our success.

Visualising makes us excited about our goals. With the Crystal Clear Principle, we looked at how to establish clear goals and a purpose. Now we envision how to map out the journey. Mapping is visualising the process, the stops on the way and our ultimate destination. As Henry Ford wisely pointed out, 'The whole secret of a successful life is to find out what is one's destiny to do, and then do it'.

Visualisation is more than just imagining. We must summon all of our senses to experience the desired result as if it were actually happening. Visualising the outcome is awesome because you can 'see' what it looks like to be there before you get there. When you do get there, it feels familiar.

Verbalise your goals

Verbalising reinforces visualisation. Athletes talk beforehand about how they intend to win a game.

Verbalising boosts our confidence and helps others to understand our purpose and why we are intent on achieving it. Confidence in ourselves inspires others to feel confidence in us, making it more likely that they will support us.

Keeping motivational quotes handy – on your desk, on the bathroom mirror, on the refrigerator, or wherever else you are likely to see them consistently – can also inspire you and keep you on track. There are many quotation sources on the internet for easy reference.

An exercise in visualisation

Take a few quiet moments to consider where you see your life in the next three to five years. Now envision it as if there were absolutely no obstacles to achieving it. Jot down on a piece of paper what you see yourself accomplishing. Give yourself free rein to envision what you can do in that time.

How does this visualisation exercise make you feel? Nervous? Sceptical? Giddy? If you are nervous or sceptical, what negative thoughts crept in to hold you back from accomplishing what it is that you dream of doing? How can you reorientate these thoughts? Feel the emotions that arise from contemplating attaining a dream without getting derailed. Does it inspire you? Do you feel motivated? Excited? How can you incorporate this into a daily visualisation to sustain those feelings of excitement and motivation?

Expectations and goals change with age. Priorities change. We may cut back on physical activity and feel our stamina levels ebb. We may no longer be able to eat whatever we want without discomfort. However, we have ideally gained expertise, wisdom, patience, character, and strength.

Keeping expectations realistic

At the end of the Stuckburies chapter, we discussed the importance of setting SMART (specific, measurable, attainable, realistic, and timely) goals. The same applies to expectations. I am not saying you shouldn't shoot for the stars; what I am saying is that your expectations cannot be realised if they are not realistic. Don't spend time visualising that you may one day win Wimbledon if you are 30 years old and have never picked up a racquet before. But, much like the story of Conor McGregor, who was on social welfare but visualised winning a UFC world title, and who trained relentlessly to achieve that dream, there are many things within your grasp if you work hard and believe in yourself. Expect the best of yourself in order to be your best.

Practise daily

Start every day before you even get out of bed visualising how successful the day is going to be and where you are going. The more you do it, the easier it becomes, and the more motivated you will feel. I start with broad visualisation before I get specific, like experiencing how I will feel once I attain the goal – the celebration, etc. I focus not just on what my goals are but what will I do and how I will feel once I get there. I imagine how this will change my life.

The more detailed I get, the more likely I am to realise what I visualise. If you do not believe it will happen, chances are it won't. We need to have expectations and take full responsibility for making them come true. The only person stopping this from happening for you is you.

Your brain visualises best when it is producing *theta* waves. You can search YouTube for theta wave music, also known as binaural beat music. Drawing and sketching also allow you to become more creative. Try using more visual words and phrases when you express yourself. Paint pictures with your words.

Affirmations

'An affirmation is a strong, positive statement that something is already,' according to Shakti Gawain, author of *Creative Visualisation*. Declaring that something is a reality before it is one creates an expectation, be it negative or positive. Fostering a positive belief generates a positive mental attitude, and combined with affirmations and visualisation, can translate to good outcomes.

Writing down an affirmation, a positive statement, for your aspirations – what you want to manifest – is a good way to develop and train your thinking patterns. Always phrase your affirmations in the present tense, not as an aspiration. Ditch the 'I will' and 'I'll try' statements in favour of simply stating a fact. (In this case, it is stating your aspiration as if it were already a fact.) An affirmation is not a statement of something you are going to do, such as, 'I'm going to learn to skydive'. It is more about who you are and how you see and believe in yourself, in the most positive way. Stick your affirmation on the wall and read it every day. Feel it. Believe it.

Examples:

- *I am grateful for today, and I choose happiness and connection.*

- *I manifest abundance for my holiday in Thailand next year.*

- *I improve every day and I feel my body getting stronger.*

- *I make things happen, reach my monthly targets with ease, and plan for my future.*

Your confidence is enhanced by having clear expectations. Choose affirming thoughts that align with your personal beliefs. Affirmations and vision boards help provide a clear focus and appeal to you on both conscious and subconscious levels.

If you visualise failure, your mind will take you there. If you can expand your mind and visualise something that is exciting, fun, challenging, rewarding, it will have a positive effect on your behaviour.

Living example of the SEV Principle

Vinnie was a general manager at a bank. Because he did not enjoy his job, he drank quite heavily, and so his girlfriend left him.

Vinnie wanted to write music. Working long hours had always got in the way of his dream. He took some leave and realised his life was not in line with his passions or sense of purpose. He had been following everyone else's expectations.

Vinnie found it easy to visualise having a music career. His dreams were never going to be achieved whilst working at the bank. His payout afforded him getting a part-time job in a music store.

Even though Vinnie swapped a life of relative comfort and financial security to become a musician, he felt on top of the world for the first time in his life. He stopped drinking and smiled more. He took his savings and went to Europe to be amongst the right people to promote his music. He struggled, but continued to visualise becoming successful in the music industry.

Eventually, Vinnie met a producer. Vinnie recognised that his expectations and visualisation were coming together because he believed in himself. By placing himself in the right environment, he attracted the right people. Vinnie got a record contract that enabled him to continue his dream and purpose.

Periodically reviewing your expectations and re-evaluating your goals to keep them achievable is part of staying successful. If you are too focused on one outcome it can be detrimental. Having a selection of strategies and options keeps your goals achievable. It is also valuable to talk to someone about your ideas – a trusted friend, a mentor, or fellow members of a mentoring group.

SUMMARY

- Happiness and expectations are linked. To be happy, we must be in tune with our expectations.

- Visualisation is a powerful tool for success, so powerful that it can trigger the same physiological reactions in the body as a real experience can.

- If we visualise a behaviour, we are more likely to perform it. Mapping allows us to visualise the stops on the way, as well as our destination.

- The SEV Principle, Select, Expect, Visualise, is about consciously selecting your thoughts and expectations and visualising the desired outcome, putting you in a position to take advantage of the opportunities that life has to offer.

- By believing in your abilities and managing your expectations, other people will find themselves drawn to your enthusiasm and excitement.

- Expectations should be realistic, not out of reach.

Principle 5: The 'Do Unto Others' Principle

> *Do unto others as you would have them to unto you.*
>
> Luke 6:31

No matter how good our intentions and how polite we might be, there are the inevitable unpleasant encounters with people who are brusque, indifferent, rude, or downright volatile. You might simply have caught them at an unfortunate moment, or having a bad day, or they might be like that all the time and not realise that their demeanour puts people off.

When people push your buttons

The majority of the time when we encounter unpleasantness, the other person is under stress or is unhappy with their current situation, perhaps even with their life as a whole. Reminding yourself of that possibility before reacting in kind, or being reactive in any way, is the first step to defuse such an encounter.

The next thing you should ask yourself is whether you may have done something, if not deliberately then unintentionally or subconsciously, to provoke such a reaction from them. Could it be that other people find *you* annoying?

Be conscious with dealings and observe the body language of others in order to be more aware and considerate. When dealing with challenging or frustrating people, try and ascertain their circumstances. Why are they presenting in this way? What is going on for them? Is it situational or are they just unaware that they can be annoying?

- If someone is overbearing, they may feel self-conscious and overcompensate.

- If they are rude and frequently interrupt, they may have poor listening skills, or even low self-esteem. They may often feel unheard.

- They might be struggling at home, going through a bitter divorce or custody battle, or be having a particularly tough time with a colleague or person of authority. If feeling frustrated, they may have no patience for pleasantries.

- Someone who is normally agreeable may come across moody and aloof. They may have just found out that someone they love has cancer. They may feel emotionally overwhelmed or numb, preoccupied.

- You wave at your neighbour from across the supermarket, and she stares at you without smiling. You feel slighted, when in fact she has misplaced her glasses and does not recognise you.

- A woman is introduced to a man who is an Orthodox Jew. She holds out her hand to shake his, unaware that his religion prevents him from doing this. Instead of explaining, he simply ignores her hand. She feels awkward and is put off by what she perceives to be rudeness, not realising she has encountered a cultural difference.

When we remind ourselves that there are always details we are unaware of, we can prevent ourselves from being too quick to judge. The way you react to someone at face value is a judgement you make about them, one not necessarily fair or accurate. The other person has a background story.

Each of us brings with us into that moment the totality of our personal experiences, such as our current mood, past history, current situation, and positive or negative expectations.

Successful people are patient people and understand that we connect at different levels and have multiple things going on. Being considerate will win attention and gain cooperation.

Anger

Deepak Chopra says, 'Anger is remembered pain'[47]. Anger stems from our childhood stuckburies and the blockages we built up as a result.

By not dealing with our blockages, we risk long-term pain and consequences. Certain people or situations may ignite our blockage, resulting in a flash of anger. More often than not, when we feel sudden anger towards someone, it is not about them but the thoughts in your head that you associate with them.

When we empathise with people's situations, we view their behaviour in a different light. We all have stuff going on in our lives. Unfortunately, there is no communication template that fits all personal situations and circumstances. We have to deal with our experiences and emotions. Understanding and adapting to someone's needs can prove a more thoughtful and seasoned approach than trying to change them.

Anger is not always a bad thing, as it is designed to help us to establish boundaries. The American Psychological Association says that anger is a completely normal and healthy human emotion. The problems associated with it arise only when anger gets out of control and becomes destructive, physically, mentally, and/or emotionally. At that point it can create a host of difficulties in any, sometimes all, aspects of our life.

The key to handling anger is to determine what lies at the root of it. If we simply ignore or suppress a feeling of anger, it will keep returning until it is resolved. Often, it stems from feeling threatened. Anger erupts when we feel we lack control in a particular circumstance. We feel weakened, and therefore want to raise our position to dominate and take immediate control. Unfortunately, when we feel angered by people or events, we think and act from a powerless mindset.

When we fail to resolve our anger, we resign ourselves to an almost continual level of stress, as our anger simmers below the surface. And that continual level of stress takes a toll. Stress can have a lasting, negative impact on the brain. A few days' exposure to stress compromises the effectiveness of brain neurons. Weeks of stress can damage brain cells, and months of stress can permanently destroy neurons. When stress gets out of control, your brain and performance suffer. When your performance suffers, so does your chance to achieve success.

Google

In 2009, Google began looking into what made a good boss. According to Adam Bryant's *The New York Times* article 'Google's Quest to Build a Better Boss', the vice president of Google's human resources department, Laszlo Bock, stated that it had been assumed that in order to be an effective manager, you needed to be a more skilled technical expert than the people working for you. It turned out that was the least important thing, that success lay more in connecting with and being accessible to your team.

Companies, particularly large corporations, understand the need for skilled human resource professionals. These professionals are well trained in how to approach and manage toxic co-workers, and have detailed policies and procedures to follow. Successful people management translates to a successful business.

Living example of the 'Do Unto Others' Principle

John was a leading electrical sales assistant who applied for a supervisory position in the bedding department. Although he knew his knowledge of electrics would be of little use, he failed to appreciate just how difficult it might be to start over. As the department supervisor, he felt embarrassed that his staff knew more than he did. He essentially closed himself off in his office to study the unfamiliar product line. He assumed his team were experienced enough to do their jobs with little or no supervision. His new staff found him unhelpful, unavailable, unapproachable, and unfriendly. Customers found him rude, as he demanded they direct their questions to staff members. His team began to show signs of wear. Morale dropped. Staff began to call out sick frequently and make less of an effort. Sales dropped, management noticed, and expressed their displeasure.

Feeling humiliated, John resigned and took a job with an electrical department at a different retailer, returning to his comfort zone.

John could have been a great manager if he had been able to let go of his fears and learnt to communicate and understand his staff's needs. He mistakenly thought that by letting his team operate independently, it conveyed his confidence in their ability to get their jobs done. Instead, they felt shut out.

When you engage with people, knowing that they want to be seen and acknowledged, it gives you the opportunity to be more open and allow yourself to be seen in the same way. And when you are clear in establishing your vision and in setting boundaries, staff and co-workers feel more at ease. They can make decisions based on mutual understanding and have expectations as to how to respond.

DISC Profiling

DISC Profiling is a leading personal assessment questionnaire, based on the work of psychologist William Moulton Marston, designed to help you to understand your and other people's behavioural traits. It enhances teamwork, reduces conflict, enables you to manage people better, respond to customer styles more effectively, and increase your self-knowledge and awareness.

People fall into one of four quadrants, according to this method, D, I, S, or C.

- **D** signifies Dominance, where emphasis is placed on getting results. These people are direct and to the point, sometimes blunt, and are willing to accept challenges.

- **I** denotes Influence, where the emphasis is on persuasion, openness, and relationships. Influencers are enthusiastic, collaborative, optimistic, and eager to be heard.

- **S** indicates Steadiness, where the emphasis lies more on cooperation, dependability, and sincerity. These tend to be calm persons who are supportive and do not need to be in the limelight. S people make great staff members, as they are reliable and consistent.

- **C** stands for Conscientiousness, and, as such, these persons place greater emphasis on competency, expertise, accuracy, and quality. They tend to be detail-orientated and work well independently and autonomously, e.g., an accountant or analyst.

There is no ideal quadrant and all are equally valuable in terms of what they contribute to a team environment. The goal of tools such as this is simply to understand how to interact most effectively with the various types of people and develop productive relationships, be they interpersonal or professional, with someone you otherwise, to put it frankly, might not be able to stand, when the need for such a relationship is unavoidable. It is effective whether it concerns a colleague or a family member.

To identify which quadrant we occupy is to better understand ourselves and, as Carl Jung said, 'Everything that irritates us about others can lead us to an understanding of ourselves'. As a bonus, it is another step on the way to increasing our emotional intelligence.

Framing

Framing refers to how you frame your words when speaking, especially reacting, to someone. It is a way of saying something that inspires a certain reaction, such as a response to something you do not agree with. Framing can be either negative or positive, depending on how you choose your words. If, for example, you were to address a member of your staff about a problem, which response would evoke a more positive reaction in you?

I don't agree with you but I suppose I have to find a solution.

or

I need to give this some thought. May I have some time to come up with a solution?

Choosing our words can mean the difference between being seen as cooperative and sounding antagonistic. If we fixate on the negative and view any sort of problem as a personal criticism, we naturally react defensively and not necessarily constructively. Choosing a positive mindset means that we accept that we are not perfect, we will not be right in every situation, but that this does not make us a bad person, and that we are willing to make an effort to find a solution. This mindset significantly improves our dealings with others.

Prepare

Before approaching a difficult person, prepare by visualising the various ways the situation might unfold. Work out the best way to say what you want to say to the other person, taking into consideration their type of personality and the likely way they'll react. Protect yourself and them. You may take them by surprise with your favourable approach.

It is important to be specific, not vague or too generalised, and to start gently. If, for example, a client has been negative about your team's performance, you can be direct without being confrontational:

> *Hi, Mike, I appreciate you're having some issues with my team's performance. It would be great to hear your feedback on how we can address this, and make it a win/win for us and the company.*

Sometimes, no matter how you try, certain individuals continue to frustrate. It could be that they live in fear, with many stuckburies, and react by trying to intimidate you and everyone around them. This intimidation can wear you down until you give up or plead with them for help.

> *Mike, since I started working here a year ago we have been feuding. I can't bear it anymore – it's exhausting. We can't keep working this way. I'm about ready to resign.*

What you want is to come in from a position of requesting help rather than rescue. This enables you to remain in control whilst respecting the other person. From there, you have to be patient and absorb. Listen and use the skills we have mentioned previously in the chapter. As Eleanor Roosevelt sagely put it, 'Nobody can make you feel inferior without your consent'.

> *Hi, Mike, I know we have differences of opinion, however, I want to understand why we aren't agreeing. Can we work out a way to work harmoniously together in the office?*

Ways to communicate

Great communication is when we say what we feel without attacking the other person. Negative communication involves avoidance or alienation.

Incomplete messages are a form of avoidance and can turn a small issue into a tense one. Avoidance stems from the fear of disapproval or meeting with hostility. For example, if you approach someone using the constructive example we just used ('I want to understand why we aren't agreeing. Can we work out a way to work harmoniously together in the office?'), someone who wishes to avoid dealing with the subject might wave their hand and say, 'Don't make such a big deal out of it', and walk away, leaving the situation unresolved.

Alienation, on the other hand, stems from feeling threatened. It can be accusing or sarcastic, and is often used in citing generalisations:

> *You're being ridiculous. You always blow things out of proportion.*

> *It doesn't matter what I say. You always think I'm wrong.*

Be decisive in your delivery. Show that you are honest and transparent and have nothing to hide. By being decisive, you recognise your own self-worth.

Express your needs and wants clearly. Do not hesitate or delay. If you leave communication for too long, the idea of presenting the issue becomes more daunting. You never end up carrying it out or, if you do, your delivery lacks sufficient impact because of the time elapsed.

Sometimes people are ambiguous. It may be a matter of just asking for clarification. For example, someone may be short with you on the phone. They may be grappling with personal issues, however, we may assume they are just being rude. It helps to ask for clarification before reading too much into their behaviour.

Stop the vortex – when someone is annoying or aggravating me, I try not to fall into the sea of illogical worry and blame. We have a tendency to start overthinking people and their behaviour. This intensifies and because we are anticipating the moment so much, nothing good can occur. When it happens, the mind can be clogged with worry and uncertainty. Something small can potentially turn into something big.

We have to realise that getting increasingly annoyed will not make them stop any sooner. Think of an irritating fly that keeps buzzing around you. It will keep buzzing until it dies, you kill it, or you let it escape outside. Why wait and let it continue to annoy you? What purpose does that serve?

Watch what you say and how you say it

Body language makes up about 55 per cent of effective communication. Your tone of voice conveys about 38 per cent and the remaining 7 per cent consists of the actual words you use. Be mindful of the way you stand, move, and the tone of your voice, especially with people you find irritating.

SUMMARY

- Treating others in the way you like to be treated is a good basis for communication. Engaging on a more personal level creates understanding and connection.

- When people push your buttons, ask yourself why this is and examine your behaviour towards them. You might not realise you're the annoying one.

- Being more conscious in our dealings with, and observing the body language of others, helps us to stay aware and be more considerate.

- When dealing with other people, consider boundaries and direction. When people have clarity as to the nature of the engagement, they are more at ease and operate based on mutual understanding and expectations.

Principle 6: The Gratitude and Delayed Gratification Principle

> *The struggle ends when gratitude begins.*
>
> Neale Donald Walsh

Have you ever dreamed of achieving something but felt conflicted by your current responsibilities, the fear of the unknown, or felt forced to set it aside to focus on more immediate, short-term results? For example, have you always wanted to be your own boss but current expenses and the fear of not making ends meet have kept you in the steady job with the guaranteed salary that you've had for years, and secretly always hated?

When you shop for something, do you tend to grab the first thing you see? Or do you shop around? Your answer may play a big part in your financial success.

I have a suggestion. It is called the Gratitude and Delayed Gratification Principle. This has inspired me and many others to be patient, even when at the breaking point.

Personal finance blogger Lance Cothern, in his blog Money Manifesto, writes that the general difference between those who run up personal unsecured debt, such as on their credit cards, and those in comparable situations who prefer being debt-free, is that 'the person with no consumer debt has mastered delayed gratification while the person with consumer debt has not'.[48] Cothern defines delayed gratification as being able to delay buying something until you actually have enough cash in hand to buy it and can afford it, versus splurging on it out of impulse, the minute you see it, when you know full well you do not have sufficient cash to pay for it at that moment in time.

It boils down to self-control. Do you have it? Do you pay off your credit cards every month or roll over an ever-increasing balance?

If you are tired of the car you drive, or envy someone else's new car, do you run out and buy a new one, even if it means having to take out a loan or expensive lease, despite the fact that your current car works just fine?

If you score a bonus or windfall, do you save a portion of it, maybe pay down on your mortgage or other debt, or do you run out and buy yourself a reward, such as the latest iPhone?

Back in Principle 1, I mentioned the famous Marshmallow Experiment, where children were left alone with a single marshmallow. They were given permission to eat the marshmallow but told that if they waited until the researcher returned before eating it, they could have two instead, whereas those who chose to eat it right away would not receive a second one.

Remember what happened? Some of the kids launched themselves at the single marshmallow, unable to wait another moment, whilst others wrestled with the temptation, wanting a second one but ultimately not being able to resist the one sitting in front of them. And some patiently sat, trusting in the idea that if they could wait, if they were willing to delay gratification, they would be doubly rewarded.

What is notable is that when researchers followed up on these same children, now adults, they discovered that those children who patiently waited were generally more successful, in terms of health and social skills as well as accomplishments.

Adhering to the principle of delayed gratification is critical to your success. And I'm going to teach you how to do it by using gratitude.

Gratitude motivates

Gratitude works in a way that ties together the past, present, and future. When you retrieve memories of particularly happy occasions (past) and acknowledge what you have at this moment that you are grateful for (present), it makes you more willing to be patient, delay gratification, and magnify your ultimate success down the road (future).

Good memories make us smile, which elevates our mood and gives us hope in tough situations. Reminding ourselves regularly of what it is we have in life that we are thankful for – people we love, a secure roof over our heads, a beloved pet, a hobby we are passionate about, for example – makes us more content in our current situation and less desperate for immediate, often all too short, gratification, to the point where we can take the long view and put off our momentary desires for shiny toys such as the latest electronic gadgets and think about the future.

Savers are people who are masters of delayed gratification. They know that they can spend all their cash every month on more expensive cars, computers, data packages for their state of the art smartphones, fancy restaurants, and clothing, for example, or they can stock money away in a more disciplined fashion in order to provide a secure, more worry-free future down the road.

Which do you practise?

Delayed gratification is NOT self-denial

Delayed gratification is not about self-sacrifice and doing without. It is merely postponing that sense of gratification a little while longer until the reward has a chance to grow even bigger.

Delayed gratification focuses on the power we have within, using our wisdom and tenacity to achieve greatness and fulfilment. Rather than making you feel miserable, it makes you feel fulfilled and energised. And isn't that what you want?

It is a bit like nature. You can go ahead and blow a bundle each week buying cut flowers, or you can invest a little of your time going out and working the soil, planting the seeds, nurturing the seedlings, and then wait a little while until you've got masses of flowers in your garden that you can cut and bring inside at any time. Which ultimately costs you more? And, more importantly, which gives you vastly more pleasure and satisfaction?

Patience pays off

One of the greatest things about sales is that it is ultimately about helping others. It is about listening to what they say, what they need, and figuring out the best way to help them fill that need.

By investing time in understanding your customer or client and giving thought to the best solutions for their particular situation, you create a potentially long-term relationship, one that's based on trust, that will likely generate not just one sale but future sales and referrals, which is a lot better than rushing into a quick sale of something that might ultimately prove dissatisfactory to the client. Delayed gratification is all about investment. Long-term relationships like this are the ones that pay the biggest dividends.

Psychologist David DeSteno led a research project, not unlike the Marshmallow Experiment, to uncover how gratitude might prove to be a tool to encourage economic patience.[49] Participants were asked to choose between receiving $54 on the spot or waiting another 30 days, at which point they would be given $80. In essence, they were choosing whether or not it was worth it to them to increase their take by $26, less than a dollar for each day they waited.

But before they made their decision, the participants were assigned one of three designations, happy, grateful, or neutral, asked to think about something from their past that generated that assigned feeling, and spend five minutes to jot down the associated memory.

Interestingly, the majority of those who focused on either happy or neutral thoughts elected to take the $54 that day.

In contrast, the participants who chose to think about something they were grateful for and spent five minutes reflecting on those feelings of gratitude exhibited a noticeable increase in both patience and self-control. In fact, as blogger Kate4Kim writes in her article 'The Gratitude Study: The Emotion that Raises Net Worth' on this study, 'the more gratitude the participants reported feeling, the more willing they were to wait for the larger return'.[50] And, as DeSteno himself noted, just harbouring positive feelings, as the happy-memory participants did, was not sufficient to instil patience the way gratitude did.

Which would you have chosen? Doesn't sound like much of a difference, does it? Ah, but not so fast! As blogger Kate4Kim pointed out, waiting just one month and gaining the extra $26 meant that their patience would reap an annualised return of a whopping 577.78 per cent.[51] Now that's what I call a successful decision!

Now, you might be tempted to think that because you give into temptation easily, that you might as well skip the rest of this chapter because you can't teach an old dog new tricks. Again, not so fast! Practising gratitude, which increased the willingness to be patient regarding rewards, is something we can all learn – it is more of an environmental issue than an inherent one, a nurture over nature, if you will. It is a practice that we can all undertake for just a few minutes a day. You can even do it before you get up in the morning, as a way to start each day in a positive, appreciative frame of mind.

Geoffrey James, in his Inc.com article, 'True Secret to Success (It's Not What You Think)', writes that people whose approach to life is coloured by appreciation are, by nature, focused on what is going well in their life and are not as easily devastated by failure. In contrast, people who are not grateful as a rule find it difficult to enjoy any measure of success and, worse, failure leaves them feeling angry and bitter – a bit like whether you view the glass as half empty versus half full.

James writes that if we really want to be successful, it's important to focus on feeling gratitude. Fortunately, he says, 'Gratitude, like most emotions, is like a muscle: The more you use it, the stronger and more resilient it becomes'.[52]

James suggests exercising this emotional muscle every night, before bed, suggesting that you replay the day's events in your head and isolate the positive ones, moments that either made you happy or events where you made someone else happy, in order to begin training your brain to view your days more positively.

Erika Andersen believes that people whose perspective is gratitude-based 'not only seek out more successes, they draw successes into their lives'.[53] She suggests writing the prompt 'I'm glad…' or 'I'm thankful…' on two little cards and keeping one at work and one at home in places you are most likely to see them frequently, and every time you glance at them, take a moment to finish the sentence with something you are grateful for, big or small.

The belief is that doing this regularly, several times a day, will slowly but surely re-orientate your perspective so that you not only develop a more positive outlook but also see changes in how others react and interact with you, perhaps even improvements in your overall health and closest relationships.

Grateful people bounce back quickly

With this more positive, appreciative mindset, failures are less devastating. Instead of wallowing in self-pity, we begin to see benefits in setbacks. What would you rather do, curse your failure and feel miserable or look at it objectively and ask yourself what can be learned by this experience? Indulging in self-pity is simply a waste of precious time, a form of procrastination. To succeed at something, we must stay focused and disciplined, and practising gratitude makes it easier to stay focused and disciplined, motivating us and driving our behaviour.

Winston Churchill famously said that success is 'the ability to go from one failure to another with no loss of enthusiasm'. That's what we are talking about here. By practising gratitude, we continue to move forward to that point of success that lies ahead, without getting derailed.

Living example of the Gratitude and Delayed Gratification Principle

Jim is an entrepreneur at heart, and has always dreamed of being his own boss. He chafes at having to work for someone else, and inevitably either quits in frustration or gets fired.

He finally starts his own business, but as soon as he does, obstacles start piling up. His wife gets sick and his beloved dog dies. The business is struggling, so he finds it difficult to cover his children's tuition on top of other expenses. He finds himself wrestling with the possibility that he is being selfish and should return to a regular salaried job so that his family does not have to struggle because of his choices.

One day he encounters an executive coach and confesses his fears about the future. The coach suggests that before he makes any decision about his career and business, he take some time out to focus on what in his life he's truly grateful for. The coach prompts him to name a few things right then, as they sip their coffees.

'Well, I am grateful that I call the shots in my job, that I don't have to answer to someone else, especially if I disagree with them.' The coach nods. 'What else?'

'Well, of course I'm grateful for my wife and kids, although I'm worried about them—' The coach interrupts and says, 'Just focus on the positives for a moment. Don't think about the downsides right now'. Jim thinks a moment before adding, 'I'm lucky that wake up each day doing something I love. And my health is good. I go for a run each evening to clear my head and I enjoy it'.

'Try doing this for a couple of weeks,' the coach suggests. 'Maybe think of one thing you're grateful for before you get out of bed and another when you get into the car to drive to work, and another when you're taking that nightly run and can collect your thoughts. Think back over the day and pinpoint one or two things that have gone well that day. Remind yourself why you're doing all of this.'

A single thought, a re-orientation from dwelling on the bad stuff to identifying what is going right *and* why you are grateful can mean the difference between deciding to pursue a business venture/dream life during tough times, and abandoning your dream for a less desirable path.

Journaling each day is an effective way to practise gratitude and enables you to look back and review your various thought patterns as well as what happened on any given day. If you make a point of jotting down the day's events along with a short list, even just one item, of what you are grateful for on that day, you will start to see patterns arise. You may even notice that your musings are becoming more optimistic, that setbacks and temporarily failures are not only less devastating but perhaps positive learning opportunities.

Say thank you

Client loyalty is often generated when clients feel valued by you, when they feel you appreciate them and their business. Do you make a point of thanking people when they do something that helps you? Or do you find yourself chafing instead, resenting feeling like you are in their debt?

This is another area where re-orientating your perspective and showing appreciation for others is going to help you in how you view yourself and your own life. Thanking others, and doing it on a regular basis, is a gift you give yourself.

Now, I'm not suggesting you go overboard and start thanking everyone you come into contact with. What I am suggesting is that you stay alert to opportunities to genuinely be grateful and express your thanks when appropriate.

Here's an example of the benefits of expressing appreciation. In 2011, Harvard Medical School's Health Publications published a mental health letter on their website entitled 'In Praise of Gratitude', which mentioned a study performed by researchers at the Wharton School, in which they randomly split fundraisers at the University of Pennsylvania into two groups. One group conducted their fundraising the way they always had, by telephoning potential donors and soliciting donations. The second group, operating on a separate day, was given a pep talk by the department's director and were told how grateful she was for their efforts. The employees who had been shown appreciation for their efforts made 50 per cent more calls to solicit donations than those who had not been thanked.[54]

When we become more alert to what's going on around us and being grateful, that is a form of mindfulness. It keeps our brains focused more on the present, on what's going on around us right now. And mindfulness is an excellent method to experience the pleasures of delayed gratification.

I like to occasionally wash clothes by hand and cook on low heat. It is an opportunity for me to practise patience and appreciation. I eat my food slowly and concentrate on how it tastes, and think about how grateful I am that I am able to provide this food, to cook it the way I like it, and envision how its good quality is improving and sustaining my good health. Just the act of cooking slowly rather than hastily enables me to savour the smell as it warms and relish the moment when it is ready to be eaten. That time elapsed is delayed gratification.

By allowing ourselves a little patience and appreciation, we learn how to delay our pleasure in a way that enables us to appreciate things that much more.

Walking is a great way to calm the nerves, lower anxiety, and lift your mood. It is also a terrific way to experience gratitude and delayed gratification. Walking, instead of driving, gives you more time to appreciate your surroundings, to practise mindfulness by noticing the birds in the trees or perhaps the breeze rustling the leaves, or the distinctive neighbourhood sounds that make up your world. (It also might curb any tendency to impulse shop and, instead, put off purchasing something that catches your eye, since you would have to carry all that stuff home with you!)

Delayed gratification strengthens resolve

Resilience is a key component to long-term success. When we practise gratitude, it helps us to weather setbacks better. It is human nature to react to negatives more strongly than to positives, and that's not always a bad thing. But what we are talking about here is gaining perspective, being able to step back and look at a situation and see not just the negatives but also the positives.

Heidi Reeder, PhD, university professor and author of *Commit to Win: How to Harness the Four Elements of Commitment to Reach Your Goals*, indicates that, on average, negative events affect people five times more than positive events do. However, she says, resilient people are able to lower that negative impact by focusing on what's positive in a situation instead of what's negative.

'Rather than just focusing on the downside (e.g., 'I made a fool of myself in front of the whole team') or just the upside (e.g., 'The team got to see that I am human, which will deepen our relationship'), they are able to hold *both* the positive and negative equally. This kind of emotional balance allows you to move forward with more confidence and less stress,' Reeder says.[55]

In essence, resilient people adapt to situations of all types instead of getting thrown off track.

In the same way as you would cut down a forest by chopping down one tree at a time, break large goals down into smaller parts. Again, your goals should be SMART goals, specific, measurable, attainable, realistic, and timely. Reward yourself after every milestone, taking a moment to consider how grateful you are for achieving what you have achieved and appreciating anyone else's contribution to your success, and then focus on your next goal. It is all about continuing to move forward.

SUMMARY

- Delayed gratification is putting off immediate, often impulsive desires for gratification in order to reap greater rewards down the road.

- Those who practise delayed gratification tend to be far more successful and healthier in life.

- Feeling and expressing appreciation makes us more patient, both with people and in situations, and stimulates increased willingness to practise delayed gratification.

- Delayed gratification is not about self-denial – it makes you feel fulfilled and energised.

- Use gratitude prompts throughout the day to remind yourself to stop and think about something that makes you happy.

- Practising gratitude makes it easier to stay focused and disciplined, motivating us and driving our behaviour.

- Genuine appreciative feedback can spur employees to work harder and clients to give you more business, because you make them feel valued.

- Resilience is key to long-term success, and practising gratitude can make us more resilient because it helps us not to give too much weight to what's negative.

- We can train ourselves to delay gratification with practice. Like working a muscle, it becomes stronger and easier to do with repetition.

Principle 7: The Intuition Principle

> *The only real valuable thing is intuition.*
> Albert Einstein

'Go with your gut.' How many times have you heard people say that? But, in truth, how often do we take into account our gut feelings when making important decisions? Do you listen to the little voice inside you, your intuition, telling you what to do, or what not to do? Or are you afraid to trust it because you think cold hard facts are telling you to do something else and you have no concrete evidence to support what your gut advises you to do?

Albert Einstein observed, 'The intuitive mind is a sacred gift and the rational mind is a faithful servant. We have created a society that honours the servant and has forgotten the gift'.

We are all born with intuition. Those who appear to be more intuitive simply practise listening to that voice inside themselves and trusting their own instincts in situations. More often than not, we fight against our intuition. To better understand intuition and where it comes from, let's take a quick look at how the mind works.

Of three minds

The mind may be divided into the unconscious, subconscious, and the conscious.

The conscious mind, represents only a small portion of the brain's total capability. It is 'conscious' of you and the world around you: sensations, perceptions, feelings, breathing, other people, the environment, etc. It communicates by way of thought, speech, physical movement, writing, and pictures.

The subconscious governs fresh memories and acts as a go-between for the conscious and the unconscious to connect.

The unconscious mind, is inaccessible to the conscious mind and includes memories you may have repressed, resulting in stuckburies, and those we've chosen to forget or dismissed as unimportant, such as what you had for breakfast three weeks ago last Tuesday.

These are not memories we can summon at will. However, something we hear, see, or smell can suddenly cause a recall. Have you ever felt yourself transported to a happy memory by something as innocuous as the smell of freshly baked bread? Or a song on the radio suddenly reminds you of slow dancing as a youngster with someone you had an immense crush on? The music is the trigger that allows you to tap into that otherwise buried memory.

This is not limited to happy memories. A song, for example, can just as easily summon a sad memory that clutches your heart as if it were happening right now. Your mind transports you back to that moment, whatever and whenever it was, and you vividly re-experience those past emotions. However, without that song, you would have been unable to tap into that same memory, which has lain buried since the event occurred.

The unconscious holds the information that drives our habits, how we behave, and our belief systems. The unconscious mind is what drives intuition and communicates by way of dreams, feelings, emotions, and our imagination. Whether you realise it or not, all the information collected by the conscious mind filters through to the unconscious and the resulting interpretation is coloured by our hidden memories and belief systems.

How far will your gut take you?

Intuition is not just about a gut feeling. The greater your expertise, the more likely your intuitive feelings will guide you in the right direction. It is about knowing yourself and your business or environment. It is also about maintaining objectivity so that your emotions do not enter into your decisions and cloud your thinking – in essence, to know yourself. Even Warren Buffett indulged in what he describes as his '200-billion-dollar blunder', where he let his irritation at a company's CEO filter into his decision to obtain a controlling percentage of the shares of Berkshire Hathaway in order to fire its CEO many years ago, an investment decision that ultimately cost him millions, and one he's long since regretted.

Stuckburies and blockages shut down gut feelings. If, for example, someone is abused as a child, fear and self-doubt interfere with perception, leaving them to struggle, unable to filter out past traumatic experiences. The confusing messages they received, whether about themselves or their environment, make the clarity necessary for their intuition to work correctly almost impossible to achieve.

Mindfulness and the unconscious mind

Mindfulness, is essentially acknowledging your current thoughts and perceptions without judging them as good or bad – they just 'are'. And when you practise mindfulness, it makes you more aware of when those judgements bleed in, colour your perceptions, and confuse your intuition, and better enable you to set them aside so that they do not interfere with decision-making.

The unconscious mind processes information at a speed far faster than we realise. Some refer to intuition as our sixth sense, an awareness of something not readily perceived through our other five senses, sight, smell, hearing, taste, and touch.

Have you ever walked across an unfamiliar threshold and sensed a negative vibe? Something does not feel right and it sets your nerves jangling? There are stories of people who get a sense of foreboding before boarding public transportation and decide at the last minute not to board and then later hear the plane has crashed or the train has derailed. Ever walk somewhere, whether it is a deserted city street or forest, not a single person in sight, and felt convinced that eyes are watching your every move? What about entering a room where two people are standing in silence and you instinctively know they've been fighting even though you have not seen or heard anything? Ever fall in love at first sight? Or just known in your heart that someone's lying?

How often do you shrug it off as ridiculous or irrational? And how often do you listen to that little voice? These are all indications of intuition at work. But the unconscious brain, at lightning speed, interprets signs that we do not consciously perceive, such as body language in the example of sensing tension between two persons. Somehow you just 'know'.

Francis Cholle, author of *The Intuitive Compass*, recommends three things to encourage your intuition to speak up and make its presence known to you on a daily basis, instead of just in extreme situations: 1) keep a journal, which encourages both your subconscious and unconscious minds; 2) turn off your inner critic and let your thoughts run at will, without trying to control or condemn them and, instead, let them flow without judgement (this is practising mindfulness); and 3) seek a quiet, solitary setting where you are undistracted by unwanted sights and sounds and can unleash your creativity.[56]

Follow your hunches

If you feel an urge to do something, pay attention and see where it leads you. Hunches can open new doors and bring you clarity on your path to success. Many an inventor has succeeded by being highly intuitive. They observe things around them, including people, identify where a particular need might lie (think correction fluid for typewriters or windshield wipers for vehicles), spend quiet time contemplating the best way to tackle the problem, and avoid negative thoughts and those who ridicule their attempts to try something new.

When you feel that hunch or hear that voice that urges you to do something, do it. If you cannot do it right away, then write it down and post it in a place where you'll be reminded of it regularly until you can take steps to see it through. You may amaze yourself at where it takes you.

Practise morning meditation

Take time out for quiet meditation. Set aside a quiet time to prepare for what lies ahead. As you practise this, answers will come to you. It will help you stay mentally clear and focused. The more you meditate, the more direction and confidence you will have.

SUMMARY

- We are all born with intuition; practising listening to it is like practising a musical instrument – it gets better with practice.

- Intuition is far more accurate when coupled with experience and expertise.

- The intuition is our unconscious mind communicating to us. The unconscious holds all of our memories, the majority of which we are unaware we still possess, because they are buried so deeply and because the conscious mind only makes up about 10 per cent of our mind's capacity.

- The information in our unconscious, such as childhood experiences and the belief systems that develop as a result of those experiences, drive our habits and how we behave. We view the world through the filter of this belief.

- Distressing childhood experiences that generate blockages in us distort and even block intuition.

Principle 8: The Creativity Principle

> *Creativity is seeing what everyone else has seen, and thinking what no one else has thought.*
>
> Albert Einstein

We know that exploring creativity, the process in which new ideas are transformed into reality, develops intuition. We become alive and full of energy when we are creative. We inspire and innovate, which results in a sense of pleasure and achievement. We discover new and wonderful things. Life becomes more interesting and pleasurable. And our energy is infectious.

So, let us look now at the importance of creativity itself and what we can do to boost our creativity.

Creativity and the cave man

Since the beginning of time, humans have been problem solvers and innovators. From the inspiration to create spears and other weapons designed to make hunting (and by extension surviving) easier, to discovering fire and innovating uses for it, and even creating language for communication, humans have expressed creativity. Various eras, such as the Renaissance, the Industrial Revolution, and today's tech explosion, highlight the enormous transitions that we have made as a species thanks to creativity and innovation.

Creativity is valued in business leaders as well. In 2010, IBM published the findings of its one-on-one interviews with more than 1500 corporate and public sector leaders, spanning 33 industries in 60 countries, indicating that of all the possible qualities and characteristics they possessed, roughly 60 per cent valued creativity as most important.[57] Despite this, companies do not foster environments that encourage creativity in their workers, an attitude that begins well before we enter the working world.

The education system stifles creativity

It should come as no surprise that the rigidity of educational systems and the stress on conformity blunts and even discourages creativity in students. As the artist Picasso noted, 'Every child is an artist. The problem is how to remain an artist once we grow up'. Essentially, we teach our children to suppress their creativity.

Are you familiar with TED Talks? 'TED' stands for technology, entertainment, and design, and the belief that these three fields converge in a powerful way. What was initially a one-off event became an annual TED Conference, with presenters that range from premier scientists to musicians and philosophers. It found a global audience after the first presentation was posted online in 2006. From there, the best TED content was posted free online in the TED Talks podcast series.

One of the podcast's most popular talks to date (as evidenced by more than 37 million views) has been education and creativity expert Sir Ken Robinson's 'Do Schools Kill Creativity?', posted in June 2006, in which he argues that our schools educate us to become good workers, not creative thinkers. Students who are creative, he says, become restless in the standard educational environment and instead of receiving encouragement are ignored or stigmatised.[58]

Creativity, Robinson claims, is as important in education as literacy. He says it is critical for each of us to be prepared to be wrong – to be permitted to be wrong – in order to come up with something original. And little kids, those in the realm of maybe four years old, are quite fine with being wrong. If they are not sure of something, they'll just 'give it a go', Robinson says, without fear and without embarrassment. They are still at the point where they are essentially fearless. And whilst being wrong is not the same thing as being creative, he points out that unless you are prepared to be wrong, to take a chance, you will never come up with anything original.

That sounds logical, doesn't it? However, by the time children go through school and reached adulthood, Robinson says, they are frightened to be seen as being wrong. The educational system's form of grading rewards being right (accurately reciting the facts they are taught) and punishes being wrong. Children learn quickly that being wrong is not acceptable and is seen as failure. Exams and tests are designed to judge right versus wrong, and children are tested to gauge failure versus creativity, inspiration, or innovation. Companies are also run this way, to stigmatise mistakes.

Robinson says that no matter where you are, no matter what continent, there are three elements in the educational hierarchy. At the top is Mathematics and Languages, below that lies Humanities, and below that, at the bottom, is Arts, with Arts being divided into Arts and Music and, below that, Drama and Dance. There are no children, Robinson says, being taught to dance or express themselves with the same frequency as Maths.

What's sad, he says, is that we are often steered away from what we love to do, where our true passions lie, and towards something that is seen as a better prospect for making a living. We are being trained to become workers, and the world's successful are often those who excel at academic achievement.

Living example of the Creativity Principle

Brian was an only child. Unable to spend much time outside because the neighbourhood was unsafe, he spent hours exploring his creativity through writing stories. However, he struggled in school and found it hard to focus, particularly in classes like Maths, History, and Science. He became more and more withdrawn. His teacher recommended his parents enrol him in a poetry or writing class, one in which he could explore his creativity and hone his storytelling skills. Brian loved it.

The more creative he became, the happier he was. His social skills improved, as did his overall school grades.

When his teacher told the class one day that she wanted them to write something for a national contest, Brian perked up. The students could write about anything. Brian penned a story of a tortoise who lived inside his shell, afraid to come out and see what lay beyond his safe little world until finally he screwed up the courage to emerge, face the world, and engage with others. The tortoise was Brian.

Brian won the national contest and later became a successful author, business owner, and entrepreneur, thanks to that early recognition and encouragement of his creative abilities.

Many people who graduate and get degrees remain unemployed because the academic bar continues to be set higher and higher. Once, all you needed to get a job was an undergraduate degree, a Bachelor's. These days you are often not hireable unless you have a Master's or even a Ph.D. A 2014 article in *The Sydney Morning Herald* was titled '30 per cent of graduates to be out of work after finishing degree'.[59]

Meanwhile, self-help and development books urge you to do what you love and the money will follow, to follow your passions in order to achieve true success and life satisfaction. I am here to tell you they are right.

If your strength is in numbers or you've been trained to focus on where you best function within that tight, academically oriented educational realm, it does not mean you lack the capacity to be creative. (After all, it was creative accounting that brought the global financial crisis down on our heads, but that's not the kind of creativity I'm urging you to tap.)

We have been subjected to the myth that some of us are creative, i.e., right brain individuals, and others are more meticulous and lacking in creativity, i.e., left brain folks. Instead, studies now show that we use our entire brain to create ideas and be creative. Yes, it is true that some brain functions do occur only on one side, but essentially the whole brain is used to create new ideas and theories to solve complex problems. So, you can be creative. You just need to figure out where your creative talents lie.

We all have strengths and weaknesses. We all have talents and skills to develop. Recognise and work on your goals by setting tasks and developing new skills in areas that appeal to you, even if they don't apply to your current career. This is the time to turn off the voice of your inner critic. Believe that you are creative and you will find ways to be creative.

Einstein famously said that 'knowledge is limited to all we now know and understand, while imagination embraces the entire world, and all there ever will be to know and understand'.

So, knowledge limits imagination but imagination does not limit knowledge. If we restrict ourselves simply to what we know, life and our experiences come to a screeching halt. Only when we shrug off our fears of being different, of being 'wrong', can we begin to envision something new, something innovative, something revolutionary! If Edison, and others, had limited themselves to the forms of illumination already available, we still would not light up our worlds with the flick of a switch.

It is about getting out of our comfort zone in order to create great ideas that inspire people's lives. You do not need to reach for the moon. Remember the expression, 'the best thing since sliced bread'? There was a time where buying sliced bread had not been contemplated. And yet someone focused on how great it would be to be able to buy bread sliced, or perhaps halved, and took the initiative to implement it. A simple idea that could be said to have changed lives around the world, no?

What about the invention of the paper bag rather than just wrapping items in brown paper? It is hard for us to conceive of a life where such conveniences were not readily available everywhere, but they weren't. So, can you think of something like putting training wheels on a bike for little kids that could change how you do business? How you operate in life in terms of conveniences? This is the kind of creativity I'm talking about.

Take a look around your world and identify an inconvenience or a struggle you face regularly. Could you envision something that might make the process easier, make your life easier? What are you waiting for? Go for it!

Positivity

We have talked about how a positive attitude is a key component to being successful in life. It also lies at the source of creativity, because in order to be creative we need a sense of optimism, hope, a feeling of infinite possibility. Creativity is the exploration and development of ideas, finding opportunities, strategies, and solutions.

And as positivity lies at the base of creativity, so does creativity give us the enthusiasm to produce and enhance a positive attitude. It is a self-renewing cycle. Every day is a new day when it is alive with inspiring new challenges. Being creative enhances our positive attitude and our life becomes more fulfilling.

Creativity is a journey, not a destination

There is a misconception that creativity is the invention of something totally new. Creativity is the creation of new ideas and implementing strategies based on knowledge.

Edison did not wake up one day and simply invent the light bulb. Edison made more than 1000 attempts to invent the light bulb (and he was by no means the only one working on it). Like Einstein, he was a prolific researcher. Both constantly looked for facts and figures to stimulate ideas. That is how the brain starts its creative process.

Psychologist, and scientific director of The Imagination Institute at the University of Pennsylvania's Positive Psychology Center, Scott Barry Kaufman breaks down creativity into four stages:[60]

1. *Preparing* for innovative ideas by learning, reasoning, and gathering information. Ideas do not appear out of thin air – they need facts and data to encourage them to flow.

2. Letting ideas *incubate*, by relaxing your mind and letting it wander in order to free it up to produce inspiration, often achieved by undertaking a relaxing activity, such as walking.

3. The '*aha!*' moment, when all the stuff you've learned comes together.

4. *Verifying* how best to adapt your idea to the marketplace and make it viable for users.

We must push ourselves to call upon good ideas. With practice, we train the brain to be more creative.

Productivity and creativity

Whilst being productive (generating results) is integral to success, creativity is the key to becoming productive. Creativity links things together. It allows you to bring forth strategies that shape productivity.

Productivity and creativity go hand in hand. If we live in a world where productivity and creativity work together, companies become more profitable. As Sir Ken Robinson pointed out in his TED Talk, we train to be workers, not innovators, and that companies push this agenda, demanding more and more concrete results rather than innovation, therefore taking the creativity out of the process. I'm suggesting you incorporate creativity into all your productivity.

As a society, we do not fulfil our creative potential. In a 2012 study conducted by Adobe Data in the US, UK, Germany, France, and Japan, only 25 per cent of people believe they are living up to their potential to be creative. More than 50 per cent of respondents believe that their country's educational system discourages creativity, and most indicated they were under pressure at work to be productive versus creative.[61]

Creativity = things + people

Steve Jobs, creator of Apple, said that creativity is nothing more than connecting things. Jobs believed that if you ask a person how they devised a creative solution or idea, they are more likely to shrug in embarrassment than bend your ear with the details of their inspiration. That, he says, is because the process wasn't a conscious one. 'They just saw something [and] it seemed obvious to them after a while. That's because they were able to connect experiences they've had and synthesize new things.'

Steve Jobs envisioned combining the mobile phone, the internet, and the iPod to create a smartphone, the wildly popular iPhone. Steve Jobs has been described as the man 'who brought poetry to the microchip'.

Steve Jobs was right. Creativity is all about connections, including connecting the best people to generate the best outcome. In business, you want to connect your marketing person with a great Web person, to connect your sales person to a great referral source. That's the path to success. You are a creative doer when you link ideas from various sources to become reality.

Back in Principle 6 we talked about how, as humans, we are naturally programmed to react more intensely to negative situations than positive ones. Couple that with our all-too-incessant inner critic, the one who pounces on everything we've ever done wrong, intent on not letting us forget it, and you have a whole lot of negativity circling you.

So, many of us play it safe to avoid making mistakes. But playing it safe means being less of who we are. And that's less fulfilling! We cannot free our minds to be creative and innovative if we are coming from a position of fear, of not wanting to make mistakes, of not wanting to be seen as wrong.

If, instead of focusing on the end result, we focus on the efforts we make and the advancements we've made, we are forward-thinking in terms of fighting the good fight, which energises us. We are quick to judge who are the winners and who are the losers, but we overlook the fact that both the winners and the losers were participants. All the winners battled at one point.

Failure can be defined as failing to try or advance. If we continually, creatively, find ways to improve, we will naturally be more productive. It is a matter of persisting with the creative side to become productive. If we worry about not being productive, it holds us back from being truly productive.

Ever watch a competitive tennis match? What is more boring than two players playing it safe, each waiting for the other to make an error? You get long tedious rallies filled with uninspiring ground shots. What makes for an exciting match is when a real champion-minded player steps onto the court. A champion takes chances and goes for every shot. They accept that unforced errors are part of the risk of being dynamic, of being a winner. Being dynamic is the only way to improve your game. They get creative with their shots, mixing them up: lobs, slices, topspin, drop shots, charging the net, down-the-line and cross-court winners that paint the lines. When you watch someone play like that it is exciting – it is thrilling tennis that holds your attention. You can feel the adrenaline pump.

What kind of player do you want to be?

Living example of the Creativity Principle

Back when I was working in a sales job, I was the number one sales person and financially rewarded for my efforts. I was motivated to work hard and sell, yet I was not having fun – I was not feeling fulfilled. I would get up every morning without any passion for what lay ahead of me that day. There was a little voice that told me I'd be happier if I did my own thing. I ignored it. After all, I reminded myself, my relationships and interactions with people were positive and productive. Yet, I felt stale. My energy and dynamic personality were shrivelling. I was not being my real self. I could not share my thoughts, ideas, and be creative with people.

Then came the day I could ignore it no longer. I was sitting by myself on a park bench when I realised I did not want to go to my deathbed without having tried to be something more, doing something I wanted to do, that I enjoyed doing. I had to stop living in fear and let my inner creativity emerge. And so I took that first step out of the safety zone I inhabited and into the risk-taking realm of creativity.

With a dramatically reduced income, I struggled to get my business started. People told me I was crazy to leave an industry in which I'd been so successful to start over in another. This time, I ignored those voices and, despite the perpetual struggle, I felt energetic every day in a way I'd never known before. I had never felt such purpose.

By starting my own business, I got my drive back. The zing returned to my voice. I wanted to help people and became more involved and engaged.

It is about choosing the right path, the right environment, for you, one that will bring out and enhance your total personality. That's the point where energy, vitality, and positivity burst out.

As Picasso once observed, 'When I was a child my mother said to me: "If you become a soldier, you'll be a general; if you become a monk, you'll be the pope." Instead I became a painter and wound up as Picasso'.

Practise self-belief to be creative

Trying, stumbling, picking yourself up again and dusting yourself off and moving forward again develops in you a strong sense of self-belief and trust. That is the key to unlocking your creative abilities.

Believe in yourself and try new and unexplored avenues. I'm suggesting that you take to heart Robert Frost's famous words in the closing of his poem 'The Road Not Taken'. In it he talks about facing the choice of taking one of two roads, convinced that he would not be passing that way again in order to later take the other. He chose the grassy one, the one that looked less worn, less travelled, and declared that choosing to go that far less popular way had 'made all the difference'.

Trust yourself to find your way. You know yourself better than anyone else does. Stop listening to and blaming everyone else. It is time to take responsibility for your own choices, your own path, for your freedom to be yourself.

Persistence

Thomas Edison said it best: 'Genius is 1 per cent inspiration and 99 per cent perspiration'.

Creativity is not just inspiration; it is being willing to stick it out, to put in the effort. Many of us are all too willing to give up at the first sign of obstacles rather than continue to try. Belief in yourself and your ideas helps you to get past the problems and succeed.

There are countless examples of individuals who have tried and failed before succeeding, and succeeding enormously. Henry Ford and Walt Disney, as well as several U.S. presidents and scores of other struggling entrepreneurs, went bankrupt. Disney was allegedly fired from the newspaper where he worked because the editor declared he lacked imagination and had no good ideas. Think of that the next time someone tells you your ideas are no good. If you believe in your ideas, you will see them through.

Get into creative mode

A 2015 study performed by the University of North Carolina's School of Medicine demonstrated that a low dose of a 10-hertz electric current enhances alpha brain wave activity and boosts creativity by as much as 7.4 per cent in healthy adults. Mindfulness training, meditation, and aerobic activity also produce alpha waves.[62]

There are many focus music albums on YouTube that you can listen to which are designed to stimulate creativity. One recent craze is colouring books for adults, some of which have hit bestseller lists.[63]

Constructive feedback

Soliciting constructive feedback is an excellent stimulator for creativity, building confidence as well as competence. Constructive feedback is not the same as telling someone what you know they want to hear. Feedback needs to be honest and delivered by people who genuinely want to help you be the best you can be. So avoid both the negative naysayers and the over-the-top flatterers.

Creative training programs also enhance creative performance, encouraging different perspectives, new ways of seeing things. Break routine by taking a different route or mode of transport to work to coax your mind to work in different ways and get the creative juices flowing.

SUMMARY

- Creativity is where ideas transform into reality. Creativity inspires passion and energy.

- Today's educational systems are geared towards 'marketable skills' and measurable results. They do not encourage free thought or creativity, and view mistakes as unacceptable rather than a valuable part of the natural learning process.

- The idea that people are either left brain (methodical) or right brain (creative) is a myth. Everyone has the potential for creativity, at varying levels, and the creative process taps places throughout our brains, both left and right.

- Creativity is not the spark of inspiration; it consists primarily of sweat, learning, and effort.

- Being positive and having a strong self-belief opens the door to creativity. Creativity is about the journey; it is not the destination.

- Creativity consists of four phases: preparation, incubation, illumination, and verification.

- Alpha waves are present when your brain idles in a default state conducive to creativity. Daydreaming, aerobics, and practising mindfulness and meditation all boost alpha waves.

Principle 9: The Taking Responsibility Principle

> *In the long run, we shape our lives, and we shape ourselves. The process never ends until we die. And the choices we make are ultimately our own responsibility.*
>
> Eleanor Roosevelt

Have you ever been stuck on a task at work? Perhaps someone needs to assist you because you do not have enough skills. You may have had a disagreement with your partner and are waiting for them either to take the blame or make the first move. You may be passionate about something yet choose to wait for the world to change. Something is broken, so you go without, because you are waiting for someone else to fix it.

Arguably, the biggest obstacle to becoming successful is waiting for something to happen or someone else to take responsibility. You may know someone who speaks often of a dream they have, however, after 20 years they still have not done anything about them – the artist who dreams of creating the priceless painting but has not quite yet got around to buying the canvas or the paints, or the co-worker who keeps talking about the book they want to write but are still organising their ideas, waiting for that moment of inspiration to strike.

They are waiting for *someone* or *something* to enter the picture to make it happen. We are accountable for our own success and the responsibility is ours. We do not have to be in charge of a team or engage and utilise other supporting people, but we are responsible for delivering what is in our power to deliver.

Much like we talked about in the last chapter on creativity, that wannabe artist or author has experienced the 1 per cent inspiration but has neglected to contribute the remaining 99 per cent perspiration that Thomas Edison pointed out was required to realise an idea. And that 99 per cent is 100 per cent his or her responsibility.

Responsibility – accountability – is key to success. A responsible person is someone whom a boss can rely on, who does not require supervision. No one wants to deal with someone unreliable. No one wants to deal with someone who, when things do not get done, makes excuses or points the finger at others.

Responsibility, on the other hand, can be shared. Picture this: four out of five sales team members hit their targets. The fifth person falls short and, as a result, the team as a whole does not obtain budget. Whilst the failing salesperson is responsible for not having attained target, it is the responsibility of the manager to fix this. A successful manager takes responsibility because he or she knows it happened under their watch, that it was their job to do what they could to correct the problem.

Great leaders take responsibility for the problems of those they lead, even when it is not directly their fault. Blame gets you nowhere. It does not fix the problem – it is not solution-orientated. It is a waste of time, but taking responsibility provides a sense of control and ownership.

Failure (except in rare occurrences) is not fatal. Failure is often a path attempted on the route to success, a path that we learn does not lead us where we want to go but helps direct us to where we should go. Failure is helpful if we can see the valuable lessons to be learned from it. As the saying goes, what does not kill you makes you stronger.

As author Rosabeth Moss Kanter observed in her October 2010 column in the Harvard Business Review, this is a new era of responsibility, one where it's 'no longer good enough to do your job well, satisfy customers, and generate financial returns'.[64] Segments of the workforce no longer work independently of each other and skate along without taking responsibility for the whole process.

One classic example, she points out, is what happened to former CEO Tony Hayward, who ran BP at the time of the devastating *Deepwater Horizon* oil rig disaster in the Gulf back in 2010. Hayward immediately pointed fingers at contractors in order to limit his company's liability and attempted to cover up the severity of the leak. (Two years later, it still leaked.) By trying to avoid blame instead of taking responsibility and taking steps to right the wrongs, Hayward proceeded to blow up his career after the public and the US government expressed outrage at his actions.

These days, we are not only expected to do a good job at work on our own tasks but also be great team members, solid support staff, and be responsible for supplies arriving on time, etc. We multitask a whole host of responsibilities.

In the past, if you went to a shoe store, the sales assistant was required to know about the shoes and how to correctly size your foot. Today, that same sales assistant needs to stay informed on when stock is scheduled to arrive, about competitors' products, about shoe marketing, and even the administration side of the sales. They need to understand how to track the client and stock control, warranty issues, and any number of factors.

Active vs. Passive

A lot of people view their lives as something that happens to them. They take no responsibility for their situation and do not realise that they can choose (or, alternatively, are too lazy) to step up to wheel and steer for themselves. But if you do not take responsibility to figure out where you are and where want to be and how you will get there, how can you ever successfully get to where you want to be?

You are not only responsible for what you do but for what you choose not to do. If you make a conscious decision to shirk responsibility, you are responsible for what happens as a result.

For example, if you studiously avoid seeing a doctor, then you are responsible for that decision and all the potential health risks that come along with avoiding screenings and preventive medicine. If you see a problem at work, even if it is a task that someone else is assigned to do and you see it is not being done right and you know what can go wrong if it continues and you fail to speak up, you are as responsible for the eventual negative outcome as the person who failed to do the task correctly.

Here is another example. Speed cameras and speed limit signs caution us to drive safely and within the rules of the road. If we choose to ignore those reminders and are caught speeding, the responsibility for that lies with us. It is not the policeman's fault, or the other drivers, or that of the terrain. You are solely responsible. Accept what you did, make a positive, proactive choice to do better next time and obey the safety rules, and move on. It is behind you and no one is there to berate you except that voice inside your head, your inner critic. Nothing shuts up that inner critic faster than when you take responsibility for your mistakes.

What such people fail to appreciate is how empowering it is to take responsibility. Why would you want to hand over control of all or a part of your life to someone else? Would you not rather keep that control for yourself? Do you think someone else will have your best interests at heart to the degree that you yourself do? I doubt it.

Living example of the Taking Responsibility Principle

Ted is the Sales Manager for a large pharmaceutical business that has recently begun to struggle. The sales team are failing to hit targets, so when Ted receives a contract from a large potential client, rather than give the lead to his sales team to convert, he decides to tackle it himself.

He negotiates a deal he feels confident will boost the company's sales to target level. The deal is significant, a once in a lifetime shot. Ted envisions the team cheering him as a hero. However, upon returning to the office, it dawns on him that he made a huge mistake with the buy price. Instead of being a win, it represents a further loss for the company. It is too late to change the deal as the contracts have been all signed.

At their sales meeting, Ted speaks the truth and takes responsibility. He lists the mistakes he feels he made and what he will do differently in the future.

Instead of blaming Ted, his colleagues and sales team feel empathy towards him for admitting he made a mistake. One by one, each member of the sales team and support staff claims responsibility for their role in the predicament the company is in.

When we accept responsibility for our choices, we demonstrate strength. In the above example, even if the team did not stick by Ted, he was quick to admit and learn from his mistake. But by assuming responsibility, Ted changes the focus of the meeting. Everyone leaves feeling more motivated to lift their performances so the company will hit budget.

To say that you are accountable for something means that you accept the consequences of your actions. However, being responsible is a more proactive, more overarching, more forward-looking term. It encompasses your willingness to drive home a goal.

Imagine that you are an auto mechanic. In terms of being accountable, you accept that you are liable for the mistakes you make in repairing any given vehicle. If anything goes wrong or you fail to do something correctly, you will be held accountable.

However, in terms of being responsible, you extend that liability to the future, to any cars that you repair whilst working in this position. Your responsibility extends beyond that which you've already done and towards what you intend to do in the future, and that includes how you interact with customers, how you will take care of the company's tools, etc.

Steve Jobs is not remembered for the precise tasks he undertook, or how rich he was. He is remembered as a global visionary in terms of how technology can be used more effectively. Richard Branson will be remembered for how he has impacted people's lives with a new, fresh, fun attitude towards flying. This is what the greatest leaders in history do: they take responsibility and make significant contributions to their community and the world.

They take responsibility. They put the lives and wellbeing of their people first. When people feel safe, amazing things happen. Their impact and results far outweigh the traditional values that are predicated on the bottom line. They know that when people do not feel safe, they fear each other and organise themselves according to their fear. Things get done only because they have to get done, not because they should be done.

All this stems from responsibility at the top. If great leaders see people who struggle within the team, they take responsibility to upskill, support, and serve as a leverage for them. Staff know they are valued and have a responsibility, not only to the company but to the cause of the leader. They work together to help each other and take responsibility for the outcomes.

To take responsibility for your life and outcomes means to not point the finger at others in order to dodge responsibility. If you do not like an outcome, then before you can effectively choose a different action to take, you must first decide what it is about that outcome that does not work for you. Change that and you are free to move on.

The core problem with blaming others, aside from dishonesty, destructiveness, and almost inevitable discovery, Peter Bregman notes in a blog post on the Psychology Today website, is that 'Blame prevents learning'. When you do not admit that you are at fault, he says, there is no motivation for you to change how you operate. You continue to make the same mistakes going forward, and that leads to more finger pointing down the road in order to continue to cover your tracks. 'It's a cycle that almost always ends badly,' he writes.[65]

Taking responsibility is proactive and constructive. Even when negative consequences result, when you accept your role in what happened, it conveys trustworthiness. Would you trust someone who studiously avoids taking the blame for anything?

Do you blame others? If you do, it is conceivable it may be a habit that grew from avoiding punishment doled out by your parents or caregiver. That said, I am not saying that you should focus on blaming a caregiver for why you blame others for your mistakes! What I am saying is that, as with all stuckburies, it can be helpful to examine where the behaviour came from *in order to change it*.

If blaming others was done to avoid repeated punishment as a child, particularly unfair or unduly harsh punishment, remind yourself that you are no longer a child. No parent is standing over you now, ready to wield a stick, metaphorical or otherwise. When you blame someone else, you place yourself in the role of victim. And someone who sees themselves as a victim is not an empowered person. They have just handed control over their own wellbeing to someone else.

That is not what successful people do.

Successful people accept that they make mistakes and they move on, determined not to repeat their mistakes. They also know that if they make mistakes and admit to them, it is all part of the learning process. If they become fearful of making mistakes, it brings on paralysis.

Decision-makers know and accept that not every decision they make will be correct. There is risk involved. You cannot know how something will turn out until you try. But the more decisions one makes, the more likely the majority of them will be right. It boils down to practice. The more you do something and learn from what you do, the more expertise you gain and the more successful you become at it.

Once you discover just how empowering and liberating taking responsibility is, you will feel your life ratchet forward. Remember, there's no such thing as standing still – either you move forwards or you move backwards. Successful people move forwards.

SUMMARY

- Taking responsibility for mistakes is an opportunity to learn. It empowers us, as it keeps us moving forwards.

- If you wait for something to happen or circumstances to change, then you abdicate responsibility over your own life.

- People who accept responsibility for their actions are seen as trustworthy; those who are evasive are seen as dishonest.

- Those who blame others when things go wrong occupy the role of victim. Successful people do not see themselves as victims. They feel in control of their choices and the circumstances in which they find themselves. They seek solutions, not excuses.

Principle 10: The Self-Analysis Principle

> *The only way to make a spoilt machine work again is to break it down, work on its inner system and fix it again. Screw out the bolts of your life, examine and work on yourself, fix your life again and get going.*
>
> Israelmore Ayivor

The 10th and final principle in the Success 1010 Programme centres on taking progress reports on how you are doing and objectively gauging them to see how far you've come, and whether you are going in the right direction or need to tweak your compass points.

This is not about self-criticism, trying to find fault with yourself, and it is certainly not about giving your inner critic free rein to beat you up about the decisions you've made or the actions you've taken, or not taken; it is about refining your journey. It is a key part of the learning process to become successful.

When you pour every ounce of your being into a venture and it fails or stagnates, it's easy to blame the world, the marketplace, consumers/customers, the economy – just about anything beyond your control – for the reasons your efforts have failed to bear fruit. We can be understandably blind to the role we unwittingly play in such failure.

The challenging approach involves intense self-scrutiny. This requires us to not only challenge our beliefs and assumptions but also take action based on how we do business. The goal of this rigorous inward-looking approach is to develop new way of thinking about our lives and goals. That begins with identifying our stuckburies and accepting why they arose in the first place, that is, a defence against childhood experiences that were traumatic, confusing, irrational, or damaging to our self-esteem. Only then can we take the necessary steps to become healthier individuals, better equipped to interact in more constructive ways. Once we do this, we can more objectively analyse what else might be holding us back.

The self-analysis principle is about becoming a better version of yourself, and that takes lots of practice and brutal self-examination. Like managing a business, we need to learn how to manage ourselves by questioning our values, performance, and contribution.

If you change the way you see things, you change the way your brain processes information, and that affects both your reactions and results. Self-analysis is something you learn by doing, by putting it into practice, not just reading about it. You may find it helpful to consult with a skilled therapist or executive coach to learn effective ways to self-analyse.

Self-analysis can be painful. However, it is worth doing. And anything worth doing is worth doing well, as the saying goes. Rather than making you feel depressed, it empowers you. You feel energised when you take positive steps to better yourself, and see the world and life from a renewed perspective.

Think of it as visiting a new city and you get lost. Instead of panicking and trying to retrace your steps, you change your perspective and no longer see yourself as having got lost. Now you are on a new adventure. You sit down at a cafe and talk to the people at the table next to you. You ask them what they love about their city and what they would recommend you do and see. It is seeing their city through their eyes, not yours. You want to view your life and yourself through a different perspective.

Try this

Journaling is an excellent tool for self-analysis. It is not necessary to write reams and reams, unless you prefer to. Simply jotting down bullet point-style notes is sufficient.

Journaling as part of self-awareness is an introspective (inward-looking) process, so start by finding a quiet place where you can be alone and undisturbed. Turn off any television, radio, and the telephone, including your mobile phone.

Spend a few moments quietly contemplating your life. Ask yourself: are you happy? Do you feel confident and upbeat as a rule but are perhaps experiencing a short spell of unhappiness or dissatisfaction? Or do you seem to feel unhappy most or even all of the time, perhaps convinced that bad things keep happening to you through no fault of your own?

Jot down how you feel, what your general mindset tends to be, and how you typically respond to situations. How do you respond when someone criticises you? What about when your boss says he/she is not happy with your work? How do you react when a stranger is brusque with you? What about when someone you know is suddenly the recipient of good fortune?

Think about all of these kinds of situations (and more) that evoke a strong response in you and note any patterns in your behaviour. Do you take things personally? Or do you take things in stride?

Do not berate yourself – this is not about finding fault, remember. It is about taking a hard, objective look at yourself, the way a stranger might, and assessing your strengths and weaknesses so that you can decide what you would like to change about yourself that might make you a happier and more successful person.

Do you feel inadequate? Do you tend to judge others harshly, perhaps diminishing their accomplishments in order in a misguided attempt to make yourself feel better? Do you find yourself muttering things like, 'Ryan is such a show-off', or 'Derek is just lucky'? These types of comments are a form of envy, which we talked about in Blockage 5, on the negativity blockage.

When you jot these things down, do so without judgement. Are you a glass half-empty kind of person? Is the grass greener on someone else's side of the fence? Do you hold up other people's successes as the measuring stick for yours? We are all on different paths, with different skills, talents, and abilities. Pause and consider what there is in your life that you are grateful for. (Review the gratitude and delayed gratification chapter again, if you need to.)

What kinds of activities lift your spirits? Do you feel better when you get those endorphins into play through exercise? When was the last time you picked up a good book that you enjoyed so much that you became totally immersed in it? Maybe cooking, trying out a new recipe, does the trick. (Shopping does not count as an activity here, as it has the potential to become addictive and possibly destructive. Limit these activities to things that can be done at little or no financial cost, unless you are comfortably off and enjoy things like boating, which can be more expensive.)

How often can you engage in these activities? Once a week, a few times a week, daily? Set yourself a goal, an achievable realistic goal, to make time for activities that give you pleasure for a few hours each week.

Have you taken time yet to set down your SMART (specific, measurable, attainable, realistic, and timely) goals for how you envision your future? If not, try doing that now.

I once encountered a homeless lady who was a prolific writer. Every time I saw her, she was writing something. Curious, I finally asked what she was writing. 'Business ideas,' she said. She told me that every day she would write down a new idea for starting a business. Writing down these ideas kept her thinking positively – it gave her hope for the future. After that, every time I passed by and saw her writing, we'd exchange knowing grins and I'd give her the thumbs up.

Then came a time when I no longer saw her. I felt badly, wondering what had happened to her. And then one day I spotted her behind the wheel of a car, wearing a business suit. I watched as she drove away, wholly focused on where she was going. I turned and stared until the car disappeared from sight. She had done something amazing, through determination, positivity, and creativity. I have never forgotten that moment, or that woman.

Questions to ask yourself

The questions I have added in this section are prompts to get you thinking more deeply about yourself. Feel free to adapt them or create your own.

What are the main blockages that stop me from being successful?

What stuckburies, the incidents from my childhood (or any period where I suffered rejection, a significant blow to my self-esteem that has caused me to doubt myself, or emotional trauma) that may have caused these blockages to develop?

Success is built upon four essential elements: faith, family, community, and work. Answer these questions to the best of your ability in each category.

Faith

What is my purpose in life?

What can I do to achieve it?

What can I do to strengthen my spirituality?

How intuitive am I, and what can I do to become more intuitive in my life?

What do I need to do, physically and mentally, to become a better version of myself?

Family

How can I become more focused and balanced with my family?

What are two things I can do every week to spend more quality time with my loved ones?

What's one thing that I can do to improve our relationships?

Community

How can I contribute to society to make a difference in people's lives?

How might I make a total stranger feel joy?

Work

What can I do over the next month to improve my performance and output at work?

How can I help someone within my job or business to get better results and make their job more fulfilling?

What are two things I can do to complete my most important project quickly?

Success principles

What is my purpose in life?

What steps will get me there?

When do I feel most creative? How can I include that in other elements of my life?

What are two things I am grateful for in life?

Which three success principles will best enable me to become and stay successful?

How can I use these to be and stay successful?

Empathy

A part of self-awareness is having empathy, not just for others but for ourselves. That is what I mean by accepting your stuckburies as existing, and understanding why they developed, and then accepting that they no longer serve you well and that it is time to change those belief systems you've been using as armour to protect yourself from hurt.

Self-help author Marianne Williamson puts an interesting spin on the Golden Rule, where we are told to love others as we love ourselves. She points out that many of us grow up having no clue how to love ourselves. And if we cannot love ourselves, how can we love others?

So a big part of this self-awareness journey is learning to see who you are for what you are, and learning to accept and love yourself. Only then can you change the things about you that you feel need to change in order to be happier, because you are doing it for the right reasons – to please yourself. And when you are happier, you relate better to others, which only increases your level of happiness and life satisfaction.

It takes time, no question. None of us are willing to abruptly put down our armour and weapons and go forth, vulnerable, simply because someone else tells us to. And we do not have to try and change everything we think needs fixing all at once. Small, steady steps, with lots of practice, is how you do it. Slow and steady wins the race, as the fable tells us. And it is all about the journey, not the destination.

Take Brian, for instance. Brian is lonely, and has not had a girlfriend in a number of years. He has come to realise that he needs to lose 15 kilos, most of which he's put on because he's been lonely and depressed. He adopts a strict diet and exercise plan, and in order to stick to his goal, he decides he won't go out socially until he has lost the 15 kilos. At that point, he is convinced he will feel more confident and can meet someone and start a relationship.

It is great that Brian is so determined to lose weight, but he needs to live his life fully in the process. Cutting himself off from meeting new people is not the answer. Instead, Brian needs to tackle some self-analysis and see what it is about how he responds to and interacts with people that might be putting women off. It might have nothing to do with his weight. As well, his frustration at feeling lonely may make him become angry inside, feeling that he's denying himself pleasure more than ever in order to lose those 15 kilos, making losing the weight an unhappy experience instead of a constructive one.

It is about looking at the whole picture, you as a whole person, and not explaining away your lack of success by pointing to things outside of you, such as assuming a potential partner would not be interested in you because you aren't buff enough.

How you relate

When you interact with someone, do you listen to them? Or do you, however unintentionally, monopolise the conversation? Are you focused more on what you want to say and less on hearing what they have to say? Do you keep one eye on them and one eye on your phone? Worse, are you skimming text messages or social media instead of paying attention to the person you are with?

One of our primal needs is to feel heard. One of the greatest gifts you can give to others is to shut up and listen, and look at them attentively when you do so. (This is particularly true in sales. Sales is about providing something to someone who needs it, and you cannot grasp what they need if you are not listening. Let the customer talk!)

If you are not sure whether you are a good listener, here's a good technique to try: mirroring. That means when someone tells you something, such as a problem they have, instead of blurting out the solution to fix everything, repeat what they've said to clarify (and demonstrate that you have been listening).

For example, if your colleague is upset because he has been taken to task for being late one too many times to work and complains that his boss does not understand that he has to take the kids to school, and how congested the traffic always is, making it hard both to get the kids there on time and himself to work on time, how would you respond? Would you say something like, 'You're right, he's a pretty insensitive jerk. I've had my own problems with him. Did I ever tell you about when…' Suddenly, it has become all about you.

If you mirrored, which makes the other person feel heard, you might say instead, 'Wow, that's rough. So he's telling you that you have to find a way to be at both places on time regardless of how difficult it is? Is there any way your spouse could take them on the days where you have to get to a meeting on time? Could you propose a flexible schedule so that you make up the time on the other end and keep him posted in advance of what days you might be a bit late?'

Focusing on the other person and what they have to say not only boosts your relationship with that person but also boosts how they view you. Put away the phone and give them your undivided attention. Unplug.

This is particularly important if you have children. Give them what they crave most – your attention, your focus. That will go a long way in preventing their developing their own stuckburies.

Find a mentor

Self-analysis does not only have to involve you. In fact, soliciting feedback from someone you think highly of, who perhaps personifies the kind of person you'd like to be, is an excellent method of bolstering your self-discovery process.

It is important to choose someone who is positive-minded and wants to see you succeed. It is also important not to choose someone who is critical or, conversely, will tell you what you want to hear instead of the truth. Hearing about ourselves and where we might be falling short is not easy. Do not make it harder by asking for input from someone who is not invested in your success in some way. Successful people are not threatened by others who wish to be successful.

The idea here is to find out how someone else sees you and take those observations to heart. As humans, we can be instinctively blind to our own selves whilst holding others up to higher standards when in fact the only one we should be holding up to a higher standard is our own self.

In sales, I never get upset when I am rejected. It inspires me to get better, work harder, pay attention more, and make changes in how my relationship with that client works. Life is like a sales rate sheet – the more things you try, the more you learn. The more you learn, the more strength you gain. The more strength you gain, the happier you become. By strength, I'm referring to controlling yourself and creating your destiny.

Do what you are meant to do, and live and love every minute of it.

SUMMARY

- Successful people are not afraid to step outside of themselves and take a rigorous look at where they may fall short, to examine their beliefs and assumptions to see what has derailed their success.

- Self-awareness requires us to look beyond the external factors that account for our lack of success, and look closely at ourselves, to challenge our assumptions and beliefs about what we do and why.

- If we change how we view things, we change our approach to tackling things.

- Journaling is an effective tool in self-assessment. Jot down not just facts but our emotions when we encounter situations, such as resistance, and then examine them closely to see whether they serve us well.

- Empathy for ourselves is as important as empathy for others. When we learn to like ourselves, it is easier to be less judgemental of others.

- People want to be heard. Listening is a skill that is too often neglected or undeveloped. We are often unaware of how little attention we pay to what people say, and instead focus either on what we want to say or on distractions like social media and mobile phones.

- Finding a mentor supports the self-analysis process, and enables us to learn more about ourselves when we solicit feedback.

Success1010™ for living.
The END and just the BEGINNING…

The goal of this book has been to set you on a course forward, to power you through life, challenging yourself, growing, contributing, and being the best version of you that you can be.

By examining success, you have given considerable thought to what success personally means to you. You now look at the various areas in your life that may be out of balance and need attention.

You've hopefully taken a hard look back at your childhood to discover what stuckburies may have given rise to blockages. Whilst uncomfortable, even painful, you have glimpsed how this opens up your world to new and greater possibilities. Greatness does not lie in being blocked.

You have read, and perhaps re-read, the 10 basic principles that underlie success, principles that help you to stay on track, motivate you, and inspire you daily, to stay on the success road and keep being amazing.

So, where to from here?

Success1010 for living, is all about challenging yourself. You may fail, but that's alright. Failures are nothing more than learning opportunities. And now you have the tools to veer you away from negativity on your way to become and stay successful.

I want you to wake up every morning eager to fulfil your purpose every day, willing to shift outside your comfort zone and feel uncomfortable for a while. That feeling of newness and awkwardness is you as you develop further as a person. Embrace it.

Living a great life is about finding and pursuing your purpose. The answers to the questions we ask ourselves throughout the process provide us all the clues we need. The better the questions, and the more honest the answers, the better informed we are.

True success is found in loving your life.

Get ready to live your dream life and be loved.

Bibliography and Suggested Reading

Achor, Shawn, 'Positive Intelligence', Harvard Business Review, Jan–Feb 2012 issue. Available at https://hbr.org/2012/01/positive-intelligence. Accessed Oct. 12, 2015.

Adams, Linda, 'Learning a New Skill Is Easier Said Than Done', Gordon Training International [n.d.]. Available at http://www.gordontraining.com/free-workplace-articles/learning-a-new-skill-is-easier-said-than-done. Accessed May 10, 2015.

Amir, On, 'Tough Choices: How Making Decisions Tires Your Brain', Jul. 22, 2008. Available at http://www.scientificamerican.com/article/tough-choices-how-making. Accessed Oct. 6, 2015.

Andersen, Erika, 'How Feeling Grateful Can Make You More Successful' Nov. 27, 2013, Forbes. Available at http://www.forbes.com/sites/erikaandersen/2013/11/27/how-feeling-grateful-can-make-you-more-successful.

April, Kurt A. et al., 'Impact of Locus of Control Expectancy on Level of Well-Being', Review of European Studies (2012), vol. 4, no. 2. Available at http://dx.doi.org/10.5539/res.v4n2p124.

Artelt, Cordula, J. Baumert, N. Julius-McElvany and J. Peschart, 'Learners for Life: Student Approaches to Learning, Results from PISA (Programme for International Student Assessment) 2000' (2003), Organisation for Economic Co-Operation and Development, p.73. Available at https://www.mpib-berlin.mpg.de/Pisa/LearnersForLife.pdf.

Bailey, Mark, 'Sports Visualisation: how to imagine your way to success', *The Telegraph*. Available at http://www.telegraph.co.uk/men/active/10568898/Sports-visualisation-how-to-imagine-your-way-to-success.html.

Bergland, Christopher, 'Alpha Brain Waves Boost Creativity and Reduce Depression: Increasing alpha brain waves can stimulate creativity and minimize depression', PsychologyToday.com, Apr. 17, 2015. Available at https://www.psychologytoday.com/blog/the-athletes-way/201504/alpha-brain-waves-boost-creativity-and-reduce-depression. Accessed Nov. 4, 2015.

Bergland, Christopher, 'The "Right Brain" Is Not the Only Source of Creativity', PsychologyToday.com, Sep. 17, 2013. Available at https://www.psychologytoday.com/blog/the-athletes-way/201309/the-right-brain-is-not-the-only-source-creativity. Accessed Oct. 1, 2015.

Bergland, Christopher, 'The Neuroscience of Madonna's Enduring Success', PsychologyToday.com, Sep. 7, 2013. Available at https://cdn.psychologytoday.com/blog/the-athletes-way/201309/the-neuroscience-madonnas-enduring-success. Access date Nov 1, 2015.

Birney, R.C., H. Burdick, and R.C. Teevan, 'Fear of Failure,' (1969), New York: Van Nostrand-Reinhold Company.

Body and Soul, 'More stressed than ever? Living in the 21st century is reportedly twice as stressful as living in the 1960s'. Available at http://www.bodyandsoul.com.au/sex+relationships/wellbeing/more+stressed+than+everr,7721. Accessed Oct. 7, 2015.

Bradberry, Travis, '12 Ways Successful People Handle Toxic People', Entrepreneur.com, Mar. 17, 2015. Available at http://www.entrepreneur.com/article/243913.

Bradt, Steve, 'Wandering mind not a happy mind: About 47% of waking hours spent thinking about what isn't going on', Harvard Gazette, Harvard University, 11 Nov. 2010. Available at http://news.harvard.edu/gazette/story/2010/11/wandering-mind-not-a-happy-mind. Accessed Oct. 5, 2015.

Bryant, Adam, 'Google's Quest to Build a Better Boss', Mar. 12, 2011, The New York Times. Available at http://www.nytimes.com/2011/03/13/business/13hire.html?_r=0. Accessed Oct. 20, 2015.

Canfield, Jack, *The Success Principles: How to Get from Where You Are to Where You Want to Be*, HarperCollins, New York (Dec. 2006).

Carey, Benedict, 'In Battle, Hunches Prove to Be Valuable', *The New York Times*, Jul. 27, 2009. Available at http://www.nytimes.com/2009/07/28/health/research/28brain.html?_r=0.

Chadwick, Kushla, 'What to Do If You Have a Fear of Success'. Available at http://www.lifehack.org/articles/communication/what-you-have-fear-success.html. Accessed Oct. 5, 2015.

Chamorro-Premuzic, Tomas, 'You Can Teach Someone to Be More Creative', Harvard Business Review, Feb. 23, 2015. Available at https://hbr.org/2015/02/you-can-teach-someone-to-be-more-creative. Accessed Apr. 1, 2015.

ChangingMinds.org, 'Locus of Control', [n.d.]. Available at http://changingminds.org/explanations/preferences/locus_control.htm. Accessed Sep. 20, 2015.

Cherry, Kendra, 'The Big Five Personality Traits: 5 Major Factors of Personality', Psychology.About.com, updated Jan. 10, 2016. Available at http://psychology.about.com/od/personalitydevelopment/a/bigfive.htm.

Chicago Sun-Times, 'Reaching out: South African school for girls born out of Oprah's need to 'feel' a connection', Jan. 2, 2007.

Cholle, Francis P., 'What Is Intuition, and How Do We Use It?', PsychologyToday.com, Aug. 31, 2011. Available at https://www.psychologytoday.com/blog/the-intuitive-compass/201108/what-is-intuition-and-how-do-we-use-it. Accessed Nov. 1, 2015.

Chopra, Deepak, M.D. and Rudolph E. Tanzi, Ph.D., *Super Brain: Unleashing the Power of Your Mind to Maximize Health, Happiness, and Spiritual Well-Being*, Harmony (reprinted Oct. 2013).

Chopra, Deepak, M.D., *The Seven Spiritual Laws of Success: A Practical Guide to the Fulfillment of Your Dreams*, New World Library (1994).

Clear, James, '40 Years of Stanford Research Found that People with This One Quality Are More Likely to Succeed'. Available at http://jamesclear.com/delayed-gratification. Accessed Oct. 8, 2015.

CopingSkills4Kids.net, 'Thinking Coping Brain', [n.d.]. Available at http://www.copingskills4kids.net/Thinking_Coping_Brain.html#The_neocortex.

D., Mikey, 'The Power of Having an Internal Locus of Control', FeelHappiness.com, Mar. 12, 2012. Available at http://feelhappiness.com/the-power-of-having-an-internal-locus-of-control. Accessed Sep. 19, 2015.

Dallett, Lydia, 'Practice Delayed Gratification to Achieve Financial Success', Business Insider Australia. Available at http://www.businessinsider.com.au/delayed-gratification-is-key-to-success-2014-1.

Deitch, Micaela, 'Dependence, Independence, Interdependence and the States in Between', 7 Habits, FranklinCovey News, Online Learning, Jun. 29, 2012. Available at http://www.franklincovey.com/blog/guest-post-dependence-independence-interdependence-stages.html.

DeSteno, David, 'Gratitude Is the New Willpower', Apr. 9, 2014, *Harvard Business Review* Available at https://hbr.org/2014/04/gratitude-is-the-new-willpower. Accessed Oct. 23, 2015.

DeSteno, David, Ph.D., *The Truth About Trust: How It Determines Success in Life, Love, Learning, and More*, Hudson Street Press, New York (2014).

DiPirro, Dani, 'make the 3-to-1 ratio of positivity work for you', PositivelyPresent.com, Jan. 25, 2010. Available at http://www.positivelypresent.com/2010/01/what-is-positivity-.html.

Dwyer, Marjorie, 'Protecting the heart with optimism: Positive thinking linked to reduced risk of cardiovascular events', Apr. 17, 2012. Available at http://news.harvard.edu/gazette/story/2012/04/protecting-the-heart-with-optimism.

Ehrenfeld, Temma, 'Why Love Is So Scary and Complicated: Three criss-crossing forces add up to "chemistry"', PsychologyToday.com, Jan. 24, 2013. Available at www.psychologytoday.com/blog/open-gently/201301/why-love-is-so-scary-and-complicated-0.

Firestone, Lisa, Ph.D., 'Fear of Intimacy: Understanding Why People Fear Intimacy', PsychAlive.org, Glendon Association, [n.d.]. Available at http://www.psychalive.org/fear-of-intimacy. Accessed Sep. 24, 2015.

Firestone, Lisa, Ph.D., 'How Your attachment Style Impacts Your Relationship: What is your attachment style', PsychologyToday.com, Jul. 30, 2013. Available at https://www.psychologytoday.com/blog/compassion-matters/201307/how-your-attachment-style-impacts-your-relationship.

Firestone, Lisa, Ph.D., 'Self-Sabotaging: Why We Get in Our Own Way', PsychAlive.org, Glendon Association, [n.d.]. Available at http://www.psychalive.org/self-sabotaging. Accessed Oct. 2015.

Firestone, Lisa, Ph.D., 'Self-Esteem vs. Narcissism, PsychAlive.org, Glendon Association, [n.d.]. Available at http://www.psychalive.org/self-esteem-vs-narcissism. Accessed Oct. 8, 2015.

Firestone, Robert, Ph.D., 'How to Stop Playing the Victim Game: Challenging negative voices is the way to overcome a victimized orientation', PsychologyToday.com, Apr. 30, 2013. Available at https://www.psychologytoday.com/blog/the-human-experience/201304/how-stop-playing-the-victim-game.

Fraley, R. Chris, 'A Brief Overview of Adult Attachment Theory and Research', University of Illinois, 2010. Available at https://internal.psychology.illinois.edu/~rcfraley/attachment.htm.

Fredrickson, Barbara, 'Are You Getting Enough Positivity in Your Diet?', *Greater Good: The Science of a Meaningful Life*, University of California, Berkeley, Jun. 21, 2011. Available at http://greatergood.berkeley.edu/article/item/are_you_getting_enough_positivity_in_your_diet.

Fredrickson, Barbara, *Positivity: Top-Notch Research Reveals the 3-to-1 Ratio That Will Change Your Life*, Harmony (2009).

Gallo, Amy, 'How to Work with Someone You Hate', *Harvard Business Review*, Jan. 30, 2012. Available at https://hbr.org/2012/01/how-to-work-with-someone-you-h. Accessed Oct. 20, 2015.

GoodTherapy.org, 'Locus of Control', updated Aug. 11, 2015. Available at http://www.goodtherapy.org/blog/psychpedia/locus-of-control. Accessed Sep. 19, 2015.

GratitudePower.net, 'The New Science of Gratitude', [n.d.]. Available at http://gratitudepower.net/science.htm.

Gravotta, Luciana, 'Be Mine Forever: Oxytocin May Help Build Long-Lasting Love: The hormone oxytocin increases empathy and communication, key to sustaining a relationship between mates', Scientific American, Feb. 12, 2013. Available at http://www.scientificamerican.com/article/be-mine-forever-oxytocin.

Gregoire, Carolyn, '10 Things Highly Intuitive People Do Differently', The Huffington Post Australia, Mar. 19, 2014, updated Apr. 29, 2014. Available at http://www.huffingtonpost.com.au/2014/03/19/the-habits-of-highly-intu_n_4958778.html?ir=Australia. Accessed Nov. 4, 2015.

Halvorson, Heidi Grant, 'A Second Chance to Make the Right Impression', Harvard Business Review, Jan.–Feb. 2015. Available at https://hbr.org/2015/01/a-second-chance-to-make-the-right-impression. Accessed Oct. 15, 2015.

Hanson, Rick, Ph.D., 'Confronting the Negativity Bias: Humans evolved to be fearful since that helped keep our ancestors alive', PsychologyToday.com, Oct. 26, 2010. Available at https://www.psychologytoday.com/blog/your-wise-brain/201010/confronting-the-negativity-bias.

Hart, Anna, 'Is a six-figure salary bad for your health?', *The Sydney Morning Herald*, Aug. 26, 2015. Available at http://www.smh.com.au/business/workplace-relations/is-a-sixfigure-salary-bad-for-your-health-20150825-gj7pua.html.

Harvard Health Publications, 'In Praise of Gratitude', Nov. 1, 2011, Harvard Mental Health Letter, Harvard Medical School. Available at http://www.health.harvard.edu/newsletter_article/in-praise-of-gratitude.

Harvard Health Publications, 'What Causes Depression?', Harvard Medical School, Jun. 9, 2009. Available at http://www.health.harvard.edu/mind-and-mood/what-causes-depression.

Harvard Women's Health Watch, 'The health benefits of strong relationships', Harvard Health Publications, Harvard Medical School, Dec. 1, 2010. Available at http://www.health.harvard.edu/newsletter_article/the-health-benefits-of-strong-relationships.

Hatter, Kathryn, 'What Are the Effects of Inconsistency in the Home Environment on Kids', Demand Media, EveryDayLife.GlobalPost.com, [n.d.]. Available at http://everydaylife.globalpost.com/effects-inconsistency-home-environment-kids-22885.html.

Holson, Laura M., 'We're All Artists Now', *The New York Times*, Sep. 4, 2015. Available at http://www.nytimes.com/2015/09/06/opinion/were-all-artists-now.html?_r=0. Accessed Nov. 4, 2015.

InfiniteMinds.info, 'Why do we start but not finish?', InfiniteMinds.info, [n.d.]. Available at http://infiniteminds.info/Consciousness-Engineering/Why-do-we-start-but-not-finish.html. Accessed Sep. 19, 2015.

Integrated Wellness.com.au, 'The Role [of] Our Three Brains', [n.d.]. Available at http://integratedwellness.com.au/articles/three-brains.

James, Geoffrey, 'True Secret to Success (It's Not What You Think)', Jul. 18, 2012, Inc. Available at http://www.inc.com/geoffrey-james/gratitude-true-secret-to-success.html.

James, Matthew B., Ph.D., 'Conscious of the Unconscious: Work with your unconscious, rather than trying to browbeat it into submission',

Jul. 30, 2013, PsychologyToday.com. Available at https://www.psychologytoday.com/blog/focus-forgiveness/201307/conscious-the-unconscious. Accessed Oct. 25, 2015.

Kanter, Rosabeth Moss, 'It's Time to Take Full Responsibility', *Harvard Business Review*, Oct. 2010. Available at https://hbr.org/2010/10/column-its-time-to-take-full-responsibility, Nov. 5, 2015.

Kets de Vries, Manfred F.R., 'Are You a Victim of the Victim Syndrome?', Faculty and Research Working Paper, INSEAD, 2012. Available at http://www.insead.edu/facultyresearch/research/doc.cfm?did=50114.

Knott, Matthew and Heath Gilmore, '30 per cent of university graduates to be out of work after finishing degree', Jun. 4, 2014, *The Sydney Morning Herald*. Available at http://www.smh.com.au/federal-politics/political-news/30-per-cent-of-university-graduates-to-be-out-of-work-after-finishing-degree-20140603-39gxv.html#ixzz3qObyLEwf.

Kobler, A. L., and Scotland, E., 'The end of hope: A social-clinical study of suicide'. New York: Free Press of Glencoe (1964).

Kotler, Steven, 'The Innovation Turbo-Charge: How to Train the Brain to Be More Creative', Forbes.com, Jul. 28, 2014. Available at http://www.forbes.com/sites/stevenkotler/2014/07/28/the-innovation-turbo-charge-heightened-creativity-with-flow/#22d58280d874. Accessed Nov. 1, 2015.

Laslocky, Meghan, 'How to Stop Attachment Insecurity from Ruining Your Love Life', Feb. 13, 2014. Available at http://greatergood.berkeley.edu/article/item/how_to_stop_attachment_insecurity_from_ruining_your_love_life.

Lefcourt, H.M., 'Locus of Control: Current Trends in Theory and Research'. NJ: Lawrence Erlbaum Associates. 1976.

LiveScience.com, 'US Military Seeks Sixth Sense Training', Mar. 6, 2012, Live Science. Available at http://www.livescience.com/18850-military-sixth-sense-soldiers-intuition.html.

Locke, Connson Chou, 'When It's Safe to Rely on Intuition (and When It's Not)', *Harvard Business Review*, Apr. 30, 2015. Available at https://hbr.org/2015/04/when-its-safe-to-rely-on-intuition-and-when-its-not. Accessed Oct. 31, 2015.

Maidique, Modesto A., 'Intuition Isn't Just about Trusting Your Gut',

Apr. 13, 2011, *Harvard Business Review*. Available at https://hbr.org/2011/04/intuition-good-bad-or-indiffer.

Marano, Hara Estroff, 'Our Brain's Negative Bias: Why our brains are more highly attuned to negative news', PsychologyToday.com, Jun. 20, 2003. Available at https://www.psychologytoday.com/articles/200306/our-brains-negative-bias.

Marks, L. I. (1998), Deconstructing Locus of Control: Implications for Practitioners. Journal of Counseling and Development, 76: 251–260. doi: 10.1002/j.1556-6676.1998.tb02540.x.

Martin, Ben, 'Fight or Flight', [n.d.], PsychCentral.com. Available at http://psychcentral.com/lib/fight-or-flight.

Mendoza-Denton, Rodolfo, Ph.D., 'Why We Self-Sabotage Our Success: We self-handicap to protect our self-esteem in difficult tasks', PsychologyToday.com. Available at https://www.psychologytoday.com/blog/are-we-born-racist/201104/why-we-self-sabotage-our-success. Accessed Apr. 15, 2011.

Miller, Michael Craig, M.D., 'Unconscious or Subconscious?', Aug. 1, 2010, Harvard Health Blog, Harvard Health Publications, Harvard Medical School. Available at http://www.health.harvard.edu/blog/unconscious-or-subconscious-20100801255.

Mindset-Habits.com, 'The Human Mind – How does it all work?', May 20, 2010. Available at http://www.mindset-habits.com/conscious-subconscious-unconscious-mind.

MindTools.com (2015) 'Thought Awareness, Rational Thinking, and Positive Thinking'. Available from https://www.mindtools.com/pages/article/newTCS_06.htm. Accessed Oct. 5, 2015.

MindTools.com. (2015) 'Overcoming Fear of Failure: Facing Fears and Moving Forward'. Available from https://www.mindtools.com/pages/article/fear-of-failure.htm. Accessed Oct. 5, 2015.

Minkoff, K., Bergman, E., Beck, A. T., and Beck, R. Hopelessness, depression, and attempted suicide. The American Journal of Psychiatry, 130(2) (1973).

Morgan, Nick, 'How to Master Yourself, Your Unconscious, and the People Around You', Mar. 7, 2013, Forbes. Available at http://www.forbes.com/sites/nickmorgan/2013/03/07/how-to-master-yourself-your-unconscious-and-the-people-around-you-3. Accessed Nov. 1, 2015.

Morgan, Nick, 'Why You Should Listen to Your Unconscious mind – and What It Can Tell You', Forbes. Apr. 23, 2013. Available at http://www.forbes.com/sites/nickmorgan/2013/04/23/why-you-should-listen-to-your-unconscious-mind-and-what-it-can-tell-you, Accessed Oct. 30, 2015.

Morin, Amy, '6 Mistakes that Keep You Struggling in Life', Lifehack.org, [n.d.]. Available at http://www.lifehack.org/articles/communication/6-mistakes-that-keep-you-struggling-life.html. Accessed Oct. 5, 2015.

Murray, B., 'Food for thought: Glucose is good for learning and memory', March 2000, Monitor on Psychology, Vol. 31, No. 3, American Psychological Association. Available at http://www.apa.org/monitor/mar00/brainbox3.aspx. Accessed Oct. 8, 2015.

Ni, Preston, 'How to Increase Your Emotional Intelligence – 6 Essentials: Six Ways to Increase Your Emotional Intelligence), Oct. 5, 2014, PsychologyToday.com. Available at https://www.psychologytoday.com/blog/communication-success/201410/how-increase-your-emotional-intelligence-6-essentials.

Niles, Frank, Ph.D., 'How to Use Visualization to Achieve Your Goals', updated Aug. 17, 2011, The Huffington Post Australia. Available at http://www.huffingtonpost.com/frank-niles-phd/visualization-goals_b_878424.html?ir=Australia. Accessed Oct. 20, 2015.

Nisen, Max, 'The Most Successful People Are Extremely Hard on Themselves', Business Insider Australia, Jan. 29, 2013. Available at http://www.businessinsider.com.au/self-assessment-is-needed-for-success-2013-1. Accessed Oct. 20, 2015.

Olson, Samantha, 'Your Gut Feeling Is Way More Than Just a Feeling: The Science of Intuition' Mar. 12, 2015, Medical Daily. Available at http://www.medicaldaily.com/your-gut-feeling-way-more-just-feeling-science-intuition-325338. Accessed Oct. 20, 2015.

Ostrovsky, Oksana and Larry Ostrovsky, 'How Your Subconscious Mind Controls Your Behavior', Genius Awakening, [n.d.]. Available at http://www.geniusawakening.com/genius-brain/subconscious-mind-controls-behavior.

Parry, Lizzie, 'It's true! Optimists DO live longer: Having a positive attitude lowers the risk of a heart attack', DailyMail.co.uk, Mar. 5, 2015. Available at http://www.dailymail.co.uk/health/article-2980770/It-s-true-Optimists-live-longer-Having-positive-attitude-lowers-risk-heart-attack.html.

Perry, Susan K., Ph.D., '5 Ways to Finish What You Start (and Why You Often Don't): These 5 precautions should keep you progressing toward a goal', PsychologyToday.com, Feb. 25, 2014. Available at https://www.psychologytoday.com/blog/creating-in-flow/201402/5-ways-finish-what-you-start-and-why-you-often-dont. Accessed Sep. 19, 2015.

Pierce, Stacia, 'How to Have Intuitive Success', The Huffington Post Australia Blog, Nov. 10, 2013, updated Jan. 23, 2014. Available at http://www.huffingtonpost.com/stacia-pierce/how-to-have-intuitive-success_b_4080666.html?ir=Australia

Prince, Michael, 'Does Active Learning Work? A Review of the Research', Journal of Engineering Education, Jul. 2004. Available at http://www4.ncsu.edu/unity/lockers/users/f/felder/public/Papers/Prince_AL.pdf.

Prince, Michael, 'Does Active Learning Work? A Review of the Research', *Journal of Engineering Education*, Jul. 2004.

PsychEducation.org, '3-Brains-in-One' Brain, updated Dec. 2014. Available at http://pscheducation.org/brain-tours/3-brains-in-one-brain.

PsychologicalScience.org, 'Trust Your Gut ... but Only Sometimes', Jan. 4, 2011, Association for Psychological Sciences. Available at http://www.psychologicalscience.org/index.php/news/releases/trust-your-gut-but-only-sometimes.html.

Rankin, Lissa, M.D., '7 Stories That Will Change Your View of Human Intuition', Mar. 11, 2014, Care2. Available at http://www.care2.com/greenliving/7-stories-that-will-make-you-believe-in-miracles.html#ixzz3qeR9ayLk.

Reynolds, Gretchen, 'Want to Be More Creative? Take a Walk', *The New York Times*, Apr. 30, 2014. Available at http://well.blogs.nytimes.com/2014/04/30/want-to-be-more-creative-take-a-walk/?_r=0.

Robinson, Ken, 'Do schools kill creativity?', TED Talk, Feb. 2006.

Available at http://www.ted.com/talks/ken_robinson_says_schools_kill_creativity.

Senge, Peter M., *The Fifth Discipline: The Art and Practice of The Learning Organization*, Random House, London, Sydney (1992).

Shandrow, Kim Lachance, 'The 5 Most Popular TED Talks of All Time', Nov. 12, 2014, Entrepreneur.com. Available at http://www.entrepreneur.com/article/239672.

Shute, Valerie J., 'Focus on Formative Feedback' (2007), Educational Testing Service. Available at https://www.ets.org/Media/Research/pdf/RR-07-11.pdf. Accessed Oct. 12, 2015.

Sincero, Sarah Mae, 'General Adaptation Syndrome', Explorable.com, Jul. 10, 2012. Available at https://explorable.com/general-adaptation-syndrome.

Stanford Medical Newsletter, 'Good stress, bad stress: Research identifies health impact of different responses' (interview with Firdaus Dhabhar), Stanford University School of Medicine, Stanford Medicine.org, Fall 2012. Available at http://stanfordmedicine.org/communitynews/2012fall/stress.html.

Stillman, Jessica, 'The 4 Stages of Creativity: Forget just getting into the bathtub and waiting to yell "Eureka!" A psychologist explains the long and winding road our brains take to produce a groundbreaking new idea', Inc. [n.d.]. Available at http://www.inc.com/jessica-stillman/the-4-stages-of-creativity.html. Accessed Nov. 1, 2015.

Sweeney, Camille and Josh Gosfield, 'Secret Ingredient for Success', Jan. 19, 2013, *The New York Times*. Available at http://www.nytimes.com/2013/01/20/opinion/sunday/secret-ingredient-for-success.html?_r=1.

TheMindUnleashed.org, 'The Conscious, Subconscious, and Unconscious Mind – How Does It All Work?', Mar. 13, 2014. Available at http://themindunleashed.org/2014/03/conscious-subconscious-unconscious-mind-work.html.

University College London, 'Equation to predict happiness', Aug. 5, 2014. Available at https://www.ucl.ac.uk/news/news-articles/0814/040814_happiness_equation#sthash.NtPZu56l.dpuf.

University of Maryland Medical Center, 'Stress', reviewed Jan. 30,

2013. Available at http://umm.edu/health/medical/reports/articles/stress. Accessed Sep. 29, 2015.

University of Utah Health Care, 'Researchers Debunk Myth of "Right-brain" and "Left-brain" Personality Traits, Aug. 14, 2013. Available at http://healthcare.utah.edu/publicaffairs/news/current/08-14-2013_brain_personality_traits.php.

Walton, Alice G., 'Recovering Resilience: 7 Methods for Becoming Mentally Stronger', Mar. 2, 2015, Forbes.com. Available at http://www.forbes.com/sites/alicegwalton/2015/03/02/growing-resilience-7-strategies-to-become-mentally-stronger.

Warrell, Margie, 'Trust Your Intuition. Not Doing So Can Be Costly', Forbes.com, May 12, 2015. Available at http://www.forbes.com/sites/margiewarrell/2015/05/12/trust-your-intuition/#4dcf5cb251f1.

Wegner, Daniel M., D.J. Schneider, S.R. Carter III, and T.L. White, 'Paradoxical Effects of Thought Suppression', *Journal of Personality and Social Psychology*, 1987, Vol. 53, No. 1, 5–13.

Wegner, Daniel M., *White Bears and Other Unwanted Thoughts: Suppression, Obsession, and the Psychology of Mental Control*, The Guilford Press, New York, NY (1994).

Young, Leon, Maj., 'Battlefield intuition: It's not a mystery', Sep. 8, 2015. Available at http://www.army.gov.au/Our-future/Blog/Articles/2015/09/Battlefield-intuition.

Zenger, Jack, 'Taking Responsibility Is the Highest Mark of Great Leaders', Forbes.com, Jul. 16, 2015. Available at http://www.forbes.com/sites/jackzenger/2015/07/16/taking-responsibility-is-the-highest-mark-of-great-leaders. Accessed Nov. 5, 2015.

Zwilling, Martin, '6 Ways That Lack of Focus Can Kill Your Business', Forbes.com, Dec. 16, 2014. Available at http://www.forbes.com/sites/martinzwilling/2014/12/16/6-ways-that-lack-of-focus-can-kill-your-business/#41e7df08463d. Accessed Oct. 8, 2015.

Notes

1 Aaker, J. Rudd, M., and Mogilner, C., 'If Money Doesn't Make You Happy, Consider Time', *Journal of Consumer Psychology*, 2011, as sourced from LaPlante, Alice, 'If Money Doesn't Make You Happy, Consider Time: Forget Suze Orman. Time, not money, is your most precious resource. Spend it wisely.' Stanford Graduate School of Business, *Insights by Stanford Business,* Marketing, Career and Success, Management, April 1, 2011, accessed 10 October 2015. See https://www.gsb.stanford.edu/insights/if-money-doesn%E2%80%99t-make-you-happy-consider-time.

2 Taylor, S. 'Elation: The Amazing Effect of Witnessing Acts of Kindness,' Nov. 15, 2013, PsychologyToday.com, see https://www.psychologytoday.com/blog/out-the-darkness/201311/elation-the-amazing-effect-witnessing-acts-kindness-0.

3 Brooks, Arthur C., 'A Formula for Happiness', *The New York Times*, Dec. 14, 2013, See: http://www.nytimes.com/2013/12/15/opinion/sunday/a-formula-for-happiness.html?_r=0

4 Erikson's stages of psychosocial development, https://en.wikipedia.org/wiki/Erikson%27s_stages_of_psychosocial_development#Stages

5 McLeod, S.A. 'Attachment Theory', SimplyPsychology.org, 2009, http://www.simplypsychology.org/attachment.html (regarding the work of John Bowlby (1958), 'The nature of the child's ties to his mother', *International Journal of Psychoanalysis*, vol. 39).

6 See more at Dollard, J. and Miller, N.E. (1950), *Personality and psychotherapy*. New York: McGraw-Hill.

7 McLeod, *op. cit.*

8 AIPC/Australian Institute of Professional Counsellors, Extract, 'Trends and Statistics of the Contemporary Family', from the original article from Mental Health Social Support Specialty 'Supporting Challenged Families', Sep. 5, 2012, retrieved Sep. 10,

2015, see http://www.aipc.net.au/articles/trends-and-statistics-of-the-contemporary-family.

9   Australian Bureau of Statistics, Counts of Australian Businesses, including Entries and Exits, Jun 2010 to Jun 2014, 2 March 2015 Media Release 'The number of Australian businesses have increased', see http://www.abs.gov.au/ausstats/abs@.nsf/mediareleasesbytitle/950EC94DB899312ECA2573B00017B8F4?OpenDocument.

10 Contrasting and categorization of emotions, https://en.wikipedia.org/wiki/Contrasting_and_categorization_of_emotions

11 World Health Organization, Depression Fact Sheet No. 369, October 2015, see http://www.who.int/mediacentre/factsheets/fs369/en.

12 Mental Health Research Institute, see http://www.mhri.edu.au/depression.

13 Harvard Health Publications, Harvard Medical School, 'Exercise and Depression', June 9, 2009, see http://www.health.harvard.edu/mind-and-mood/exercise-and-depression-report-excerpt.

14 McLeod, S.A. 'Erik Erikson', SimplyPsychology.org, see http://www.simplypsychology.org/Erik-Erikson.html.

15 DiPirro, D. 'Make the 3-to-1 ratio of positivity work for you', PositivelyPresent.com, January 25, 2010, see http://www.positivelypresent.com/2010/01/what-is-positivity-.html.

16 'Locus of Control', ChangingMinds.org [n.d.], see http://changingminds.org/explanations/preferences/locus_control.htm, accessed 20 Sept. 2015.

17 Kets de Vries, M.F.R. 'Are You a Victim of the Victim Syndrome?', Faculty and Research Working Paper, INSEAD, 2012, see http://www.insead.edu/facultyresearch/research/doc.cfm?did=50114.

18 Marks, L. I. 'Deconstructing Locus of Control: Implications for Practitioners'. Journal of Counseling and Development, 1988, 76: 251–260. doi: 10.1002/j.1556-6676.1998.tb02540.x. See also Torun and April, 2006; Minkoff et al., 1973; Kobler and Scotland, 1964.

19 Lefcourt, H.M. 'Locus of Control: Current Trends in Theory and Research. NJ: Lawrence Erlbaum Associates. 1976.

20 Kurt A. April et al., 'Impact of Locus of Control Expectancy on Level of Well-Being', Review of European Studies (2012), vol. 4, no. 2, see http://dx.doi.org/10.5539/res.v4n2p124.

21 Perry, S.K. '5 Ways to Finish What You Start (and Why You Often Don't)', https://www.psychologytoday.com/blog/creating-in-flow/201402/5-ways-finish-what-you-start-and-why-you-often-dont
22 'More stressed than ever? Living in the 21st century is reportedly twice as stressful as living in the 1960s', Body and Soul, see http://www.bodyandsoul.com.au/sex+relationships/wellbeing/more+stressed+than+everr,7721.
23 Sincero, S.M. 'General Adaptation Syndrome', *Explorable*, see https://explorable.com/general-adaptation-syndrome.
24 *Ibid.*
25 *Ibid.*
26 Hatter, K. 'What Are the Effects of Inconsistency in the Home Environment on Kids', Demand Media, EveryDayLife.GlobalPost.com, see http://everydaylife.globalpost.com/effects-inconsistency-home-environment-kids-22885.html.
27 University of Maryland Medical Center, 'Stress', last reviewed January 30, 2013, see http://umm.edu/health/medical/reports/articles/stress.
28 Richter, R. '5 Questions: Dhabhar on the good and bad aspects of stress', Stanford Medicine News Center, Oct. 22, 2012, see http://med.stanford.edu/news/all-news/2012/10/5-questions-dhabhar-on-the-good-and-bad-aspects-of-stress.html.
29 University of Maryland Medical Center, *op.* cit.
30 'The health benefits of strong relationships', Harvard Women's Health Watch, Harvard Health Publications, Harvard Medical School, Dec. 1, 2010, see http://www.health.harvard.edu/newsletter_article/the-health-benefits-of-strong-relationships.
31 Temma Ehrenfeld, 'Why Love Is So Scary and Complicated: Three criss-crossing forces add up to "chemistry"', PsychologyToday.com, Jan. 24, 2013, see www.psychologytoday.com/blog/open-gently/201301/why-love-is-so-scary-and-complicated-0.
32 Lisa Firestone, Ph.D., 'Fear of Intimacy: Understanding Why People Fear Intimacy', PsychAlive.org, Glendon Association, [n.d.], accessed Sep. 24, 2015, see http://www.psychalive.org/fear-of-intimacy.
33 *Ibid.*
34 *Ibid.*

35 Albert Mehrabian, Wikipedia, https://en.wikipedia.org/wiki/Albert_Mehrabian
36 Micaela Deitch, 'Dependence, Independence, Interdependence and the States in Between', 7 Habits, FranklinCovey News, Online Learning, Jun. 29, 2012, http://www.franklincovey.com/blog/guest-post-dependence-independence-interdependence-stages.html.
37 Lisa Firestone, Ph.D., 'Self-Sabotaging: Why We Get in Our Own Way', PsychAlive.org, Glendon Association, [n.d.], see http://www.psychalive.org/self-sabotaging.
38 Lisa Firestone, Ph.D., 'Self-Esteem vs. Narcissism', PsychAlive.org, Glendon Association, [n.d.], see http://www.psychalive.org/self-esteem-vs-narcissism, accessed 8 Oct 2015.
39 Rodolfo Mendoza-Denton, Ph.D., 'Why We Self-Sabotage Our Success: We self-handicap to protect our self-esteem in difficult tasks', PsychologyToday.com, Apr. 15, 2011, see https://www.psychologytoday.com/blog/are-we-born-racist/201104/why-we-self-sabotage-our-success.
40 MindTools.com. (2015) 'Overcoming Fear of Failure: Facing Fears and Moving Forward', see https://www.mindtools.com/pages/article/fear-of-failure.htm. Accessed Oct. 5, 2015.
41 Ibid.
42 Killingsworth, M.A and Gilbert, D.T., 'A Wandering Mind Is an Unhappy Mind', http://science.sciencemag.org/content/330/6006/932.full?sid=3d27f229-6e05-4828-b560-1516e79f2a4d#ref-12
43 Zwilling M. '6 Ways that Lack of Focus Can Kill Your Business',
44 Daniel Goleman, 'Research Affirms Power of Positive Thinking', *The New York Times*, Feb. 7, 1987, see http://www.nytimes.com/1987/02/03/science/research-affirms-power-of-positive-thinking.html?pagewanted=all.
45 Kendra Cherry, 'The Big 5 Personality Traits', updated Jan. 10, 2016, About.com, see http://psychology.about.com/od/personalitydevelopment/a/bigfive.htm.
46 Sandra Mahar and Maddy Harford, 'Research on Human Learning Background Paper', Paper No. 1, Dept. Of Education and Training,

Feb. 2005, which cites C. Rogers, 'Freedom to learn: a view of what education might become', CE Merrill, Columbus, 1969.
47 Deepak Chopra, Twitter, https://twitter.com/deepakchopra/status/83512201750650880
48 Lydia Dallett, 'Practice Delayed Gratification to Achieve Financial Success', *Business Insider Australia*, Jan. 25, 2014, see http://www.businessinsider.com.au/delayed-gratification-is-key-to-success-2014-1.
49 David DeSteno, 'Gratitude Is the New Will Power', *Harvard Business Review*, Apr. 9, 2014, see https://hbr.org/2014/04/gratitude-is-the-new-willpower.
50 Kate4Kim, 'The Gratitude Study: The Emotion that Raises Net Worth', Partners4Prosperity, Sep. 25, 2014, see http://partners4prosperity.com/the-gratitude-study-on-saving.
51 Ibid.
52 Geoffrey James, 'True Secret to Success (It's Not What You Think)', Inc.com, Jul. 18, 2012, see http://www.inc.com/geoffrey-james/gratitude-true-secret-to-success.html?goback=%252Egde_4233131_member_137240558.
53 Erika Andersen, 'How Feeling Grateful Can Make You More Successful', Forbes.com, Nov. 27, 2013, see http://www.forbes.com/sites/erikaandersen/2013/11/27/how-feeling-grateful-can-make-you-more-successful/#5a04327611fd.
54 Harvard Mental Health Letter, Harvard Health Publications, Harvard Medical School, Nov. 1, 2011, see http://www.health.harvard.edu/newsletter_article/in-praise-of-gratitude.
55 Alice G. Walton, 'Recovering Resilience: 7 Methods for Becoming Mentally Stronger', Forbes.com, Mar. 2, 2015, see http://www.forbes.com/sites/alicegwalton/2015/03/02/growing-resilience-7-strategies-to-become-mentally-stronger/#22156f395a5e.
56 Francis P. Cholle, 'What Is Intuition, and How Do We Use It?', PsychologyToday.com, Aug. 31, 2011, see https://www.psychologytoday.com/blog/the-intuitive-compass/201108/what-is-intuition-and-how-do-we-use-it, accessed Nov. 1, 2015.

57 'IBM 2010 Global CEO Study: Creativity Selected as Most Crucial Factor for Future Success', IBM Press Release, May 18, 2010, see https://www-03.ibm.com/press/us/en/pressrelease/31670.wss.

58 Ken Robinson, 'Do Schools Kill Creativity?', TED Talks podcast, filmed Feb. 2006, see http://www.ted.com/talks/ken_robinson_says_schools_kill_creativity.

59 Matthew Knott and Heath Gilmore, '30 per cent of university graduates to be out of work after finishing degree', *The Sydney Morning Herald*, Jun. 4, 2014, see http://www.smh.com.au/federal-politics/political-news/30-per-cent-of-university-graduates-to-be-out-of-work-after-finishing-degree-20140603-39gxv.html#ixzz3qObyLEwf.

60 Jessica Stillman, 'The 4 Stages of Creativity', Inc.com, Oct. 1, 2014, see http://www.inc.com/jessica-stillman/the-4-stages-of-creativity.html, accessed Nov. 1, 2015.

61 Rupal Parekh, 'Global Study: 75% of People Think They're Not Living Up to Creative Potential', *Advertising Age*, Apr. 23, 2012, see http://adage.com/article/news/study-75-living-creative-potential/234302.

62 Christopher Bergland, 'Alpha Brain Waves Boost Creativity and Reduce Depression', PsychologyToday.com, April 17, 2015, see https://www.psychologytoday.com/blog/the-athletes-way/201504/alpha-brain-waves-boost-creativity-and-reduce-depression, accessed Nov. 4, 2015.

63 Laura M. Holson, 'We're All Artists Now', *The New York Times*, Sep. 4, 2015, see http://www.nytimes.com/2015/09/06/opinion/were-all-artists-now.html?_r=2, accessed Nov. 4, 2015.

64 Rosabeth Moss Kanter, 'It's Time to Take Full Responsibility', *Harvard Business Review*, Oct. 2010, see https://hbr.org/2010/10/column-its-time-to-take-full-responsibility.

65 Peter Bregman, 'Why You Should Take the Blame: Transform negatives into positives and improve your credibility', PsychologyToday.com blog post, Apr. 9, 2013, see https://www.psychologytoday.com/blog/how-we-work/201304/why-you-should-take-the-blame.

www.ingramcontent.com/pod-product-compliance
Lightning Source LLC
Chambersburg PA
CBHW070639160426
43194CB00009B/1501